HISTORY OF EDUCATION IN INDIA

HISTORY OF EDUCATION IN INDIA

UNDER THE

Rule of the East India Company

MAJOR B. D. BASU, I.M.S. (RETIRED)

SECOND EDITION

GYAN

Published by

Gyan Publishing House
5, Ansari Road
Daryaganj, New Delhi-110002
Phone: 011-47034999, 9811692060
E-mail: books@gyanbooks.com

Distribution Network
gyanbooks.com
India, USA, Canada, UK, Australia, France

ISBN : 978-81-212-9586-4 (PB)
First Published, 1867

2nd Impression 2023

Printed at: Gyan Press, Delhi.

HISTORY OF EDUCATION IN INDIA
Author:MAJOR B. D. BASU

HISTORY OF EDUCATION IN INDIA UNDER THE Rule of the East India Company

Major B. D. BASU, I.M.S. (Retired)

Second Edition

TO THE

REVERED MEMORY OF MY FATHER

SHYAMA CHARAN BASU

WHO

By the organization of the Educational Department,
By zealously supporting the cause of female education,
By the foundation of the Punjab University, and
By "throwing himself actively into all the movements,"*
Calculated to ameliorate the condition of
The people of the Punjab,
Was looked upon as one of the chief makers of
The Young Punjab.

---

* The *Indian Public Opinion* of Lahore, dated 13th August, 1867.

PREFACE

The history of education in India under British rule has yet to be properly written. It should be remembered that in the pre-British period, India was not an illiterate country. This land was far more advanced in education than many a Christian country of the West. Almost every village had its school for the diffusion of not only 3 but 4 R's—the last R being Religion or the Ramayana. That work has contributed not a little to the preservation of Hindu culture.

Stress has not been laid on another fact, which is, that educational institutions were not established in this country as soon as the East India Company obtained political supremacy here. It took the Christian merchant " adventurers " just a century to come to the decision that it was for their benefit to impart education to the swarthy " heathens " of India. The battle of Plassey was fought in 1757; and Wood's Despatch, commonly called the Educational Charter of India, is dated 1854. This would show that the system of education now in vogue in this country was not introduced in hot haste but after the mature deliberations of nearly a century. The number of those English Christians who consider that it was a mistake to have introduced Western education in this country is not a small one. But they should be reminded of the fact that the mistake was committed after nearly a century's deliberation.

It should also not be lost sight of that the Indians themselves were the pioneers in introducing Western education in this country. The Hindu College of Calcutta was established long before Macaulay penned his celebrated minute or Wood sent out his Educational Despatch to India.

It was to emphasize these facts that the preparation of this work was undertaken. It appeared originally in *The Modern Review* in the shape of serial articles, from which it is reprinted with a few additions and alterations.

CONTENTS

Major B. D. Basu

HISTORY OF

EDUCATION IN INDIA

UNDER THE

Rule of the East India Company

EDUCATION OF INDIANS—(1813-1833).

I. STATE AID.

When the East India Company attained political supremacy in India, they did not bestow any thought on the education of the inhabitants of their dominions.* Gold was their watchword. Every one of their servants who came out to India tried to enrich himself as quickly as possible at the expense of the children of the soil. It was on this account that Burke described them as "birds of prey and passage" in India. Regard-

* In the pre-British period in India, there were four methods of education at work; *viz.*, the instruction given by the Brahmanas to their disciples; the *tols*, or seats of Sanskrit learning; the maktabs and madrassas for Mohamedans; and schools in almost every village of note.

ing this class of the British sojourners in India, Burke said :

"Young Magistrates who undertake the government and spoliation of India, animated with all the avarice of age, and all the impetuosity of youth, they roll in one after another, wave after wave; and there is nothing before the eyes of the natives but an endless hopeless prospect of new flights of birds of prey and passage, with appetite continually renewing for a food that is continually wasting. * * * Their prey is lodged in England, and the cries of India are given to seas and winds, to be blown about, in every breaking up of the monsoon, over a remote and unhearing ocean. * * *

"Here (in England) the manufacturer and husbandman will bless the just and punctual hand that in India has torn the cloth from the loom, or wrested the scanty portion of rice and salt from the peasant of Bengal, or wrung from him the very opium in which he forgot his oppression and his oppressors."

According to Herbert Spencer,

"The Anglo Indians of the last century—'birds of prey and passage,' as they were styled by Burke—showed themselves only a shade less cruel than their prototypes of Peru and Mexico. Imagine how black must have been their deeds, when even the Directors of the Company admitted that 'the vast fortunes acquired in the inland trade have been obtained by a scene of the most tyrannical and oppressive conduct that was ever known in any age or country'."

These residents of Britain after making their fortunes retired to England, where they were known as "Indian Nabobs."

The Christian "Indian Nabobs" looked on the heathens of India in the same light as their co-religionists of America did on their Negro slaves. Writes a modern historian:

"But we should carry away an utterly misleading impression if we supposed that the colonial slavery of modern times reproduced the servile system of states like ancient Egypt, Babylon, and Rome. Whereas in the ancient world men of every race and rank were, owing to the fortunes of war, liable to fall into servitude, the modern planters of America and the West Indies laid violent hands on a single race—the African negroes. Moreover the labour which, under the lash, they compelled the negroes to perform was restricted to such products as rice, sugar, indigo, cotton and tobacco. In the slave states there was no attempt to teach those men any handicraft.

"On the contrary, the education of negroes was expressly forbidden. Here, for instance, are some passages from the Code of Virginia in 1849; 'Every assemblage of negroes for the purpose of instruction in reading or writing shall be an unlawful assembly. Any justice may issue his warrant to any officer or other person requiring him to enter any place where such assemblage may be and seize any negro therein; and he or any other justice may order such negro to be punished with stripes. Again, if a white person assemble with negroes for the purpose of instructing them to read or write, he shall be confined to jail not exceeding six months and fined not exceeding one hundred dollars '."

"Here is another paragraph from an Act passed in South Carolina in 1834: 'If any person shall hereafter teach any slave to read or write, or shall aid in assisting any slave to read or write, or cause or procure any slave to be taught to read or write, such person, if a free white person, upon conviction thereof, shall for every such offence against this act be fined not exceeding one hundred dollars, and imprisoned not more than six months; or if a person of colour, shall be whipped not exceeding fifty lashes, and fined not exceeding fifty dollars. And if a slave, shall be whipped not exceeding fifty lashes '." Similar acts were passed in Georgia and Alabama.

"Those Christian Legislators thus doomed the entire servile population to perpetual ignorance and degradation. Their aim was to exclude their slaves from all human and humanising influences. Contrast this policy, however, with the policy of antiquity. No doubt thousands and thousands of slaves worked and perished in chains on the harvest fields of Egypt, Babylonia, and Sicily, and in Asiatic and European copper, tin and silver mines. Their forced labour upon the raw materials of ancient industry was as severe as the labour which Christian States imposed upon the negroes of Africa in the nineteenth century. But the slave products of antiquity were not confined to agricultural and mineral wealth. There was no department of art or of industry in which servile labour was unrepresented." (Harmsworth : History of the World, Vol. IV, p. 2814).

But as years rolled on, it became patent to some thoughtful Anglo-Indians, that their dominion in India could not last long unless education —especially Western—was diffused among the inhabitants of that land. Accordingly in 1793 A.D., on the occasion of the renewal of the East India Company's Charter, an attempt was made by some people in England to compel the Company to spend a portion of the revenues of India on the education of Indians. But this proposition struck terror and dismay into the hearts of the generality of the people of England.

In his evidence on the 15th June, 1853, before the Select Committee of the House of Lords appointed to inquire into the affairs of the East India Company, Mr. J. C. Marshman said :

"For a considerable time after the British Government had been established in India, there was great opposition to any system of instruction for the Natives. The feelings of the public authorities in this country were first tested upon the subject in the year 1792, when Mr. Wilberforce proposed to add two clauses to the Charter Act of that year, for sending out schoolmasters to India; this encountered the greatest opposition in the Court of Proprietors, and it was found necessary to withdarw the clauses. That proposal gave rise to a very memorable debate, in which, for the first time, the views of the Court of Directors upon the subject of education, after we had obtained possession of the country, were developed. On that occasion, one of the Directors stated that we had just lost America from our folly, in having allowed the establishment of Schools and Colleges, and that it would not do for us to repeat the same act of folly in regard to India; and that if the Natives required anything in the way of education, they must come to England for it. For 20 years after that period, down to the year 1813, the same feeling of opposition to the education of the Natives continued to prevail among the ruling authorities in this country."

Twenty years rolled away and the Company's Charter came to be renewed in 1813. This time the attempt to make the Company set apart a fractional portion of their revenues in educating the people of India was successful. A clause was inserted on the motion of Mr. R. P. Smith, who had been Advocate-General in Calcutta, in the Charter Act of 1813, which ran as follows :

"53 Georgii 3, Cap. 155, Sec. 43. And be it further enacted, that it shall be lawful for the Governor-General-in-Council to direct that out of any surplus which may remain of the rents, revenues and profits arising from the said territorial acquisitions, after defraying the expenses of the military, civil and commercial establishments, and paying the interest of the debt, in manner hereinafter provided, a sum of not less than one lac of rupees in each year shall be set apart and applied to the revival and improvement of literature, and the encouragement of the learned natives of India, and for the introduction and promotion of a knowledge of the sciences among the inhabitants of the British territories in India; and that any schools, public lectures, or other institutions for the purposes aforesaid, which shall be founded at the presidencies of Fort William, Fort St. George, or Bombay, or in any other parts of the British territories in India, in virtue of this Act, shall be governed by such Regulations as may from time to time be made by the said Governor-General-in-Council, subject, nevertheless, to such powers as are herein vested in the said Board of Commissioners for the affairs of India, respecting colleges and seminaries; provided always, that all appointments to offices in such schools, lectureships, and other institutions, shall be made by or under the authority of the Governments within which the same shall be situated."

It was, of course, from considerations of political expediency that the magnificent sum of one lac of rupees was ordered to be set apart for the instruction of the natives of India. This is also evident from the letter of instructions communicated to the Bengal Government by the Court of Directors, an extract from which is reproduced below :

Extract from a letter, in the Public Department, from the Court of Directors to the Governor-General-in-Council of Bengal; dated 3rd June, 1814.

"In our Letter of the 6th September last, in the Public Department, we directed your attention generally to the 43rd Clause in the Act of the 53rd of the King, by which our Governor-General-in-Council is empowered to direct that a sum of not less than one lac of rupees out of any surplus revenues that may remain shall be annually applied to the revival and improvement of literature, and the encouragement of the learned natives of India. We purpose in this Despatch to convey to you our sentiments as to the mode in which it will be advisable you should proceed, and the measures, it may be proper, you should adopt with reference to that subject.

"In the consideration of it, we have kept in view those peculiar circumstances of our political relation with India which, having necessarily transferred all power and pre-eminence from native to European agency, have rendered it incumbent upon us, from motives of policy as well as from a principle of justice, to consult the feelings, and even to yield to the prejudices, of the natives, whenever it can be done with safety to our dominions.

"The Clause presents two distinct propositions for consideration; first, the encouragement of the learned natives of India, and the revival and improvement of literature; secondly, the promotion of a knowledge of the sciences amongst the inhabitants of that country.

"Neither of these objects is, we apprehend, to be obtained through the medium of public colleges, if established under the rules, and upon a plan similar to those that have been founded at our universities, because the natives of caste and of reputation will not submit to the subordination and discipline of a college; and we doubt whether it would be practicable to devise any specific plan which would promise the successful accomplishment of the objects under consideration.

"We are inclined to think that the mode by which the learned Hindoos might be disposed to concur with us in prosecuting those objects would be by our leaving them to the practice of an usage, long established amongst them, of giving instruction at their own houses, and by our encouraging them in the exercise and cultivation of their talents, by the stimulus of honorary marks of distinction, and in some instances by grants of pecuniary assistance.

"In a political point of view, considerable advantages might, we conceive, be made to flow from the measure proposed, if it should be conducted with due attention to the usages and habits of the natives. They are known to attach a notion of sanctity to the soil, the buildings and other objects of devout resort, and particularly to that at Benares, which is regarded as the central point of their religious worship, and as the great repository of their learning. The possession of this venerated city, to which every class and rank of the Hindoos is occasionally attracted, has placed in the hands of the British Government a powerful instrument of connexion and conciliation, especially with the Mahrattas, who are more strongly attached than any other to the supposed sanctity of Benares.

"Deeply impressed with these sentiments, we desire that your attention may be directed in an especial manner to Benares and that you call upon your public representatives there to report to you what ancient establishments are still existing for the diffusion of knowledge in that city; what branches of science and literature are taught there; by what means the professors and teachers are supported; and in what way their present establishments might be improved to most advantage.

* * * *

"We refer with particular satisfaction upon this occasion to that distinguished feature of internal polity which prevails in some parts of India, and by which the instruction of the people is provided for by a certain charge upon the produce of the soil, and by other endowments in favour of the village teachers, who are thereby rendered public servants of the community.

"The mode of instruction that from time immemorial has been practised under these masters has received the highest tribute of praise by its adoption in this country, under the direction of the Reverend Dr. Bell, formerly chaplain at Madras; and it is now become the mode by which education is conducted in our national establishments, from a conviction of the facility it affords in the acquisition of language by simplifying the process of instruction.

"This venerable and benevolent institution of the Hindoos is represented to have withstood the shock of revolutions, and to its operation is ascribed the general intelligence of the natives as scribes and accountants. We are so strongly persuaded of its great utility that we are desirous you should take early measures to inform yourselves of its present state, and that you will report to us the result of your inquiries, affording, in the meantime, the protection of Government to the village teachers in all their just rights and immunities, and marking by some favourable distinction any individual amongst them who may be recommended by superior merit or acquirements; for, humble as their situation may appear, if judged by a comparison with any corresponding character in this country, we understand those village teachers are held in great veneration throughout India.

"We are informed that there are in the Sanskrit language many excellent systems of Ethics, with codes of laws and compendiums of the duties relating to every class of the people, the study of which might be useful to those natives who may be destined for the Judicial Department of Government. There are also many tracts of merit, we are told, on the virtues of plants and drugs, and on the application of them in medicine, the knowledge of which might prove desirable to the European practitioner, and there are treatises on Astronomy and Mathematics, including Geometry and Algebra, which, though they may not add new lights to European science, might be made to form links of communication between the natives and the gentlemen in our service, which are attached to the Observatory and to the department of engineers, and by such intercourse the natives might gradually be led to adopt the modern improvements in those and other sciences.

"With a view to those several objects we have determined that due encouragement should be given to such of our servants in any of these departments as may be disposed to apply themselves to the study of the Sanscrit language,* *

"We encourage ourselves to hope, that a foundation may in this way be laid for giving full effect in the course of time to the liberal intentions of the Legislature; and we shall consider the money that may be allotted to this service as beneficially employed, if it should prove the means, by an improved intercourse of the European with the natives, to produce those reciprocal feelings of regard and respect which are essential to the permanent interests of the British Empire in India."*

It is evident from the letter, an extract from which has been given above, that it was not so much the intention of the Legislature to do anything in the shape of disseminating knowledge among the inhabitants of India as to make a survey of the indigenous educational institutions that existed in the country and also to take steps for their preservation. It should be remembered that India was not a country inhabited by savages and barbarians. In the pre-British period, India possessed educational institutions of a nature which did not exist in the countries of the West.

That even in the beginning of the Nineteenth Century, India, in the matter of education, was in advance of the European countries is proved by the fact of her teaching those countries a new system of tuition, to which attention was drawn

* Affairs of the East India Company, Vol. I. Published 1832, pp. 446-47.

by the Court of Directors in their letter to the Governor-General-in-Council in Bengal, dated 3rd June, 1814, extracts from which have been already given above. Very few in India know that the system of "mutual tuition"—which has been practised by Indian school-masters since time immemorial—has been borrowed by the Christian countries of the West from India. The man who first introduced it into Great Britain was a native of Scotland by the name of Dr. Andrew Bell.

The village communities of India had not then been destroyed, and it being the duty of every village community to foster education, a school formed a prominent institution in every village of any note. Thus one Mr. A. D. Campbell, Collector of Bellary, wrote in his Report, dated 1823, as follows:

"16. The economy with which children are taught to write in the native schools and the system by which the more advanced scholars are caused to teach the less advanced, and at the same time to confirm their own knowledge, is centainly admirable, and well deserved the imitation it has received in England. The chief defects in the native schools are the nature of the books and learning taught, and the want of competent masters.

"17. Imperfect, however, as the present education of the natives is, there are few who possess the means to command it for their children. Even were books of a proper kind plentiful, and the master every way adequate to the task imposed upon him, he would make no advance from one class to another, except as he might be paid for his labour. While learning the first rudiments, it is common for the scholar to pay to the teacher a quarter of a rupee, and when arrived as far as to write on paper, or at the higher branches of arithmetic, half a rupee per mensem. But in proceeding further, such as explaining books which are all written in verse, giving the meaning of Sanskrit words, and illustrating the principles of Vernacular languages, such demands are made as exceed the means of most parents. There is, therefore, no alternative but that of leaving their children only partially instructed, and consequently ignorant of the most essential and useful parts of a liberal education: but there are multitudes who cannot even avail themselves of the advantages of the system, defective as it is.

"18. I am sorry to state, that this is ascribable to the gradual but general impoverishment of the country. The means of the manufacturing classes have been of late years greatly diminished by the introduction of our own English manufactures in lieu of the Indian cotton fabrics. The removal of many of our troops from our own territories to the distant frontiers of our newly subsidized allies has also, of late years, affected the demand for grain; the transfer of the capital of the country from the native government and their officers, who liberally expended it in India, to Europeans, restricted by law from employing it even temporarily in India, and daily draining it from the land, has likewise tended to this effect, which has not been alleviated by a less rigid enforcement of the revenue due to the State. The greater part of the middling and lower classes of the people are now unable to defray the expenses incident upon the education of their offspring, while their necessities require the assistance of their children as soon as their tender limbs are capable of the smallest labour.

"19. It cannot have escaped the government that of nearly a million of souls in this District, not 7,000 are now at school, a proportion which exhibits but too strongly the result above stated. In many villages where formerly there were schools, there are now none and in many others where there were large schools, now only a few children of the most opulent are taught, others being unable from poverty to attend, or to pay what is demanded.

"20. Such is the state in this District of the various schools in which reading, writing and arithmetic are taught in the vernacular dialects of the country, as has been always usual in India, by teachers who are paid by their schools. * * But learning, though it may proudly decline to sell its stores, has never flourished in any country except under the encouragement of the ruling power, and the countenance and support once given to science in this part of India has long been withheld.

"21. Of the 533 institutions for education now existing in this District, I am ashamed to say not one now derives any support from the State. * *

"22. There is no doubt, that in former times, especially under the Hindoo Governments, very large grants, both in money and in land, were issued for the support of learning. * *

"23. * * Considerable alienations of revenue, which formerly did honour to the State, by upholding and encouraging learning, have deteriorated under our rule into the means of supporting ignorance; whilst science, deserted by the powerful aid she formerly received from Government, has often been reduced to beg her scanty and uncertain meal from the chance benevolence of charitable individuals; and it would be difficult to point out any period in the history of India when she stood more in need of the proffered aid of Government to raise her from the degraded state into which she has fallen, and dispel the prevailing ignorance which so unhappily pervades the land."

Extracts from the report of A. D. Campbell, Esq., the Collector of Bellary, dated Bellary, August 17, 1823, upon the Education of Natives: pp. 503-504 of Report from Select Committee on the affairs of the East India Company, Vol. I., published 1832.

The late Mr. Keir Hardie, in his work on *India*, (p. 5), wrote :

"Max-Muller, on the strength of official documents and a missionary report concerning education in Bengal prior to the British occupation, asserts that there were then 80,000 native schools in Bengal, or one for every 400 of the population. Ludlow, in his history of British India, says that 'in every Hindoo village which has retained its old form I am assured that the children generally are able to read, write, and cipher, but where we have swept away the village system, as in Bengal, there the village school has also disappeared '."

Regarding education in the Deccan, in the pre-British period, Mountstuart Elphinstone, in in his Minute on Education written in March, 1824, said :

"The great body of the people (of the Deccan) are quite illiterate; yet there is a certain class in which men capable of reading, writing, and instructing, exist in much greater numbers than are required, or can find employment. This is a state of things which can not long continue. The present abundance of people of education is owing to the demand there was for such persons under the Maratha Government. That cause has now ceased, the effect will soon follow, and unless some exertion is made by the Government, the country will certainly be in a worse state under our rule than it was under the Peshwas. I do not confine this observation to what is called learning, which, in its present form, must unavoidably fall off under us, but to the humbler acts of reading and writing, which, if left to themselves, will decline among the Brahmins without increasing among the other castes."

What Elphinstone anticipated has actually come to pass.

We thus see, that in all the three presidencies of Bengal, Madras and Bombay, there was a kind of mass education in the Pre-British period.

But with the destruction of the village communities and the inpoverishment of the people

2

which were inseparably connected with the British mode of administration of India, educational institutions which used to flourish in every village of note became things of the past.

The baneful effect of the administration of the British merchants constituting the East India Company was observable not only in the destruction of Indian trades and industries, but also in that of the indigenous system of education. Thus Walter Hamilton, writing in 1828 from official records, said :

> "It has long been remarked that science and literature are in a progressive state of decay among the natives of India, the number of learned men being not only diminished, but the circle of learning, even among those who still devote themselves to it, greatly contracted. The abstract sciences are abandoned; and no branch of learning cultivated, but what is connected with the peculiar religious sects and doctrines, or with the astrology of the people. The principal cause of this retrograde condition of literature may be traced to the want of that encouragement which was formerly afforded to it by princes, chieftains and opulent individuals, under the native governments, now past and gone." (Vol. I, p. 203).

The British administrators of India of those days were actuated by political motives in keeping Indians ignorant. Thus one gallant Major-

General Sir Lionel Smith, K.C.B., at the enquiry of 1831, said :

"The effect of education will be to do away with all the prejudices of sects and religions by which we have hitherto kept the country—the Mussalmans against Hindus, and so on; the effect of education will be to expand their minds, and show them their vast power."

When the framers of the Charter Act of 1813 set apart one lac of rupees, it was their intention that the Government of India would make a survey of the indigenous educational institutions and do something for their preservation. But the Indian Government did nothing of the sort. It was so late as June 25th, 1822, that is, nine years after the passing of the Charter Act of 1813, that Sir Thomas Munro in inditing a Minute in his capacity as governor of Madras was compelled to say :

"We have made geographical and agricultural surveys of our provinces, we have investigated their resources, and endeavoured to ascertain their population; but little or nothing has been done to learn the state of education. We have no record to shew the actual state of education throughout the country. Partial inquiries have been made by individuals, but those have taken place at distant periods, and on a small scale, and no inference can be drawn from them with regard to the country in general."*

* *Ibid*, p. 500.

The Indian Government did not pay any heed to the other instructions which the Court of Directors communicated to them in their letter of 3rd June, 1814. Thus the Court had written :—

"There are also many tracts of merit, we are told, on the virtues of plants and drugs, and on the application of them in medicine, the knowledge of which might prove desirable to the European practitioner."

But the Indian Government did absolutely nothing for the study of the indigenous drugs of India.

It appears that it was not the intention of the Legislature to diffuse knowledge among the mass of the people.

Thus one Mr. Fraser of Delhi

"reported to the Chief Secretary to Government in September, 1823, that considering the ignorance and immorality of the mass of the people, and actuated by a desire to improve their moral and intellectual condition, he had at different periods since the year 1814, instituted schools for the instruction of about 80 boys, children of the Zaminders, or peasantry, in reading and writing the persian language, at an expense to himself of about Rs. 200 per mensem. This institution he proposed to place under the patronage of the Government, and recommended that it should be extended so as to afford instruction in the English, Persian and Hindoo languages to 400 boys, the children of Zaminders, at an expense of Rs. 8,400 per annum.

"The general committee to whom this proposition was referred, considered the charge large in comparison with the extent of benefit to result from it, and with the village schools of Chinsurah, and objected, on general principles, to the government charging the school fund with this expenditure, remarking that fund was not equal to any extended patronage of village schools, and that as the peasantry of few other countries would bear a comparison as to their state of education with those of many parts of British India, the limited funds under the committee's management ought in preference to be employed in giving a liberal education to the higher classes of the community. The Government concurring in this opinion, Mr. Fraser was informed accordingly." *

The Court of Directors of the East India Company also concurred in this opinion. In their letter to the Governor-General in Council of Bengal, dated 5th September, 1827, they wrote:—

"From the limited nature of the means at your disposal, you can only engage in very limited undertakings; and where a preference must be made there can be no doubt of the utility of commencing both at the places of the greatest importance, and with the superior and middle classes of the natives, from whom the native agents whom you have occasion to employ in the functions of Government are most fitly drawn, and whose influence on the rest of their countrymen is the most extensive."†

---

* *Ibid*, p. 409.
† *Ibid*, p. 490.

It was political expediency which prompted the Indian Government to undertake the education of Indians. Even a very large portion of the magnificent sum of one lac of rupees was not spent for many years for the purpose for which it had been recommended to be set apart. But it was necessary to spend money on education, otherwise it was impossible to get servants for the public services of the State. Thus some of the witnesses in their evidence before the Lord's Committee of 1830 deposed that—

"The Sudder Adawlut has represented that the knowledge of the Hindoo and Mahomedan law is becoming extinct among the natives, and that there is much difficulty in finding law officers."*

The Calcutta Madrissa, or Mahomedan College was founded by Mr. Warren Hastings in 1781 "with a view, * * to the production of well-qualified officers of the Courts of Justice."†

The Benares Hindoo College was founded in 1791 with the same object in view as the Calcutta Madrissa, that is to say, to produce well-qualified Hindoo law officers for the Courts of Justice.

These were perhaps the only two educational institutions which received any support from the Government of India previous to the passing of

* *Ibid*, p. 298.
† *Ibid*, p. 369.

the Charter Act of 1813 which authorised the annual expenditure of one lac of rupees for educational purposes.

The Deccan College at Poona was established in 1821. The Peishwas used to annually distribute large sums of money among learned Brahmins. After the annexation of the Deccan to the British territory, it was proposed by Mr. Chaplin, Commissioner of the Deccan, to devote part of the funds which the Peishwas used to distribute annually to the support of a College. Such was the origin of the Poona College.

Thus the Government of India were compelled to spend some money on the education of Indians, otherwise it was impossible for them to get employes for their public services. We have said above that it was the intention of the Legislature to spend a portion of one lac of rupees per annum on the education of Indians in order to qualify them for the public services of the State. As a matter of fact, the Indian Government were gettting Indian public servants not only very cheap but without paying much for their education. The truth of this assertion will be proved to demonstration, if we take into consideration the large sums which the Governments of Bengal, Madras and Bombay had to spend every year from the beginning of the nineteenth century on the education of their Civil Servants.

There was a college established at Calcutta in 1800 for the education of Civilians. The sum of 1,50,000 rupees was fixed by the Honourable Court of Directors for the annual expenses of the College.

The following is the Memorandum, showing the average expense of the education of each writer during three years (1825-1828).

	Rs.	A.	P.
"In the year 1825-26, the expenses of the College of Fort William, exclusive of the Salaries of the students, amounted to ..	1,36,497	13	5
"In 1826-27	1,26,500	9	1
"In 1827-28	1,39,636	10	7
"Rent of the Writers-buildings for two years, at 140 rupees for each of 19 sets of the rooms in them	95,760	0	0
"Salary of 114 Students for three years, at 300 rupees per month	2,56,470	0	0
TOTAL ..	7,54,865	1	1

"And this sum divided by 114, the number of writers in three years, will give an average expense for each writer of 6,621 rupees.*

The following table† gives an account of the

* Page 644 of Appendix (L) to Report from Select Committee on the affairs of the East India Company, Vol. I. Public.

† Page 676 of Appendix (L) to Report from Select Committee on the affairs of the East India Company, Vol. I. Public.

expense attending the establishment of the College from its institution in 1800 to 1830; also the number of individuals who have received instruction there in each year :—

Year.	Expense attending the establishment of the College.	Number of Students.
1801-2	52,411	57
1802-3	51,540	40
1803-4	53,197	44
1804-5	36,665	67
1805-6	29,797	41
1806-7	18,884	38
1807-8	18,635	36
1808-9	18,456	38
1809-10	18,105	44
1810-11	20,738	45
1811-12	20,861	32
1812-13	20,172	41
1813-14	23,707	46
1814-15	23,674	49
1815-16	21,378	37
1816-17	17,204	32
1817-18	15,682	34
1818-19	15,752	29
1819-20	14,368	19
1820-21	14,489	18
1821-22	14,314	17
1822-23	15,953	16
1823-24	13,247	9
1824-25	13,240	16
1825-26	16,215	16

Year.	Expense attending the establishment of the College.	Number of Students.
1826-27	14,731	23
1827-28	15,694	38
1828-29	15,694	38
1828-29	15,895	53
1829-30	14,598	49

Regarding the College at Madras, in a letter from the Civil Finance Committee, dated 1st October, 1829, it was written that—

"The College of Fort St. George is similarly superintended by a Board, consisting of a member of Council as president, and of three other gentlemen selected from amongst those holding offices at the Presidency, attached to which are a Secretary and Assistant Secretary, on salaries amounting to Rs. 350 and 300 respectively. There are no professors or examiners attached to the institution, but, * * the translators to Government perform the duty of examiners. The native establishment consists chiefly of moonshees, retained for the purpose of affording instruction to the junior civil servants, whose salaries, regulated at different rates according to the mode in which they are employed, amount to Rs. 1,125 per mensem; the total charge on account of the institution being Rs. 1,995.8 per mensem, or including contingencies, Rs. 24,807 annually.

"At Madras, the allowance of junior civil servants on their first admission into the College is Rs. 175, which is increased progressively, on the attainment of prescribed degrees of proficiency to Rs. 260 and Rs. 350. In addition to the allowances above mentioned, each student receives the sum of Rs. 35 per mensem for house rent. * *

"One of the principal items of charges connected with the College at Calcutta, which does not exist at the presidency of Fort St. George, is the salaries of the professors, and of the pundits, etc., attached to them.

The expenses of the college at Madras were as follows :—

In 1818	..	..	58,296
1819	..	..	65,439
1820	..	..	57,880
1821	..	..	50,842
1822	..	..	47,661

In a letter from the Secretary to the Madras College to the Chief Secretary to the Government of Madras, dated 27th August, 1828, it was stated that—

"On a computation of the expenditure on account of junior civil servants attached to the College of Fort St. George from the year 1820 up to the present time, it appears that the annual expense to Government at which instruction has been afforded to *each student* may be stated at between three and four thousand rupees, the salary of the student being included in this amount: as the fluctuating number of the students prevents the

* Page 651 of Appendix (L) to Report from Select Committee on the affairs of the East India Company, Vol. I. (Public).

expenditure of one year forming any criterion whereby to judge of that of another, the Board have thought it advisable to state the actual expenditure at which instruction has been afforded to the junior civil servants attached to the College during the last three years.

Year.	Number of students attached to the College.	Amount of Junior Civil Servants' salaries and allowance drawn at the Presidency.	Amount of Junior Civil Servants salaries and allowance drawn at Out-Stations.
1825	23	42,287 4 5½	10,780
1826	26	61,349 2 3¾	6,030
1827	30	67,850 13 8	4,650

Year.	Amount of Native Teachers' salaries drawn at the Presidency.	Amount of Native Teachers' salaries drawn at Out-Stations.	Total of the year.
1825	15,176	1,104 2 8½	69,347 7 2
1826	17,972	165 0 0	85,516 2 3¼
1827	19,326	1,520 0 0	93,346 13 8

Regarding Bombay, in a letter from the Civil Finance Committee, dated 1st October, 1829, it was stated that—

"At Bombay there is no College, but the young men receive Rs. 38 per mensem for maintaining a moonshee, and are attached soon after their arrival to different collectors in the provinces, as supernumerary assistants, until they are reported ready to pass an examination. They are then examined by a committee temporarily

* Page 689 of Appendix (L) to Report from Select Committee on the affairs of the East India Company, Vol. I. (Public).

formed at the Presidency, and if they pass in one language they are promoted to the station of an assistant, but they must pass in two languages before they become eligible to the station of a second assistant. We have no alteration to suggest in the system thus generally described, as it is stated to be efficient, and is clearly economical.

At one time it was proposed to establish a college for the education of civil servants at Bombay. *Thus in the public letter from the Bombay Government, dated 29th August, 1821, it was stated that—

"The instructions conveyed by your honourable Court in the 57th paragraph of your despatch, dated the 14th of July 1819, in the Revenue Department, have introduced us to take measures for the establishment of a college at this presidency; and as the subject has occupied our serious attention during the last year, we proceed to submit our proceedings to your honourable Court. * * * *

"The establishment was to be placed under a College Council, assisted by a Secretary, who was also to be examiner and librarian.

"In addition to the salary of the Secretary of 1,000 rupees per month, the following sketch of the expense of the college comprehends the best estimate we can form of the amount, the salaries for the teachers having been fixed at the lowest possible scale; *viz.*

---

* Page 652 of Appendix (L) to Report from Select Committee on the affairs of the East India Company, Vol. I. (Public).

"The College for instructing Europeans, calculated for from 30 to 40 students:

1 Native of Arabia, for *Arabic* ..	Rs.	100
2 Natives of Persia, for *Persian* (who might also occasionally teach Arabic, if qualified,) at Rs. 100, and Rs. 80 ..	"	180
10 Teachers of Hindoostanee, average 60 (the majority might be expected to be qualified to teach *Persian*) ..	"	600
5 Teachers of Mahratta (also qualified to teach Sanscrit), at rupees 60, average	"	300
5 Teachers of Guzzerattee, qualified to teach Sanscrit	"	300
TOTAL ..	Rs.	1,480

"With regard to the establishment of a college at Bombay on the plan thus submitted to your honourable Court, we have been prevented from carrying the arrangement into immediate effect, * * but we strongly recommend the adoption of it.

"The only possible objection that appears in our minds is the expense, but the greater part of it must be incurred whether the college be eventually instituted or not, while the education of your junior civil servants is evidently indispensable; nor are we aware of any other arrangement by which this can be effectually provided for."*

In other words, the Bombay Government con-

---

* Page 693 of Appendix (L) to Report from Select Committee on the affairs of the East India Company, Vol. I. (Public).

sidered an annual expenditure of Rupees thirty thousand necessary for the instruction of some 30 or 40 European Government servants. Had the College been established, the annual expense to Government at which instruction would have been afforded to each student would have been about one thousand rupees, the salary of the students *not* being included in this amount.

But the Court of Directors of the East India Company did not approve of the Establishment of the College at Bombay. In their letter to the Bombay Government, dated 11th June, 1823, they wrote :—

"This being the view which we take of the subject, and nothing being regarded by us as essential but the teaching of these three native languages, Hindoostanee, Mahratta and Guzzerattee, we are far indeed from being of opinion that the apparatus of a College and its great expense are either required for the purpose, or would afford the best means of accomplishing the end.

"Two things alone appear to us to be necessary; the first, a sufficient number of natives qualified to teach to young Englishmen the three languages in question, the second, a well-constituted organ of superintendence for seeing that the masters perform their duty, and for examining the students."*

* Page 697 of Appendix (L) to Report from Select Committee on the affairs of the East India Company, Vol. I. (Public).

So the scheme for the establishment of the College for the instruction of junior civil servants at Bombay fell through. But nevertheless the education of the European public servants of the Bombay Government cost the Indian tax-payer as large a sum as that of Bengal or Bombay.

Now, let us see what it cost the Indian Government to educate the Indians from whom also public servants had to be recruited.

Previous to 1813, there were only two educational institutions in India, *viz.*, the Calcutta Madrissa and the Benares Hindoo Sanscrit College, which were maintained at the expense of the Indian Government. The pecuniary aid afforded to these institutions is exhibited in the follolwing tables :—

" An Abstract Statement of Pecuniary Aid, granted by the *Bengal* Government to the *Calcutta* Madrissa, from its first institution to the end of the year 1824, so far as the same can be ascertained.

	Rs.
Cost of the original building in 1781 ..	75,745
Revenue of lands granted to the institution as an endowment of the estimated value of 29,000 rupees per annum, from A.D. 1782 to 1793, 12 years ..	3,48,000
Actual expenditure from 1794 to 1818, 25 years as per account exhibited in July 1819	4,94,197

	Rs.
Charges on account of the Madrissa as fixed by Government,	
A. D. 1819	30,000
1820	30,000
1821	30,000
1822	30,000
1823	30,000
1824	30,000
Sum appropriated in July, 1823, for the purchase of ground, and erection of a new Madrissa	1,40,537
TOTAL ..	12,20,479*

"Amount of the pecuniary aid granted by the Bengal Government to the College of Benares, (including the assignments of revenue):—

	Rs.
For the year 1791	14,000
From 1st January, 1792 to 31st December, 1824, being 33 years, at 20,000 rupees per annum	6,60,000
TOTAL ..	6,74,000†

It should be remembered that not an inconsiderable portion of the above sums went into the pockets of the Anglo-Indians who were appointed as Superintendents of the above two institutions.

* *Ibid*, p. 399.
† *Ibid*, p. 40.

Thus the Superintendent of the Calcutta Madrissa used to get 6,000 Rupees and that of the Benares College 5,400 Rupees a year.

The following two tables* are very important.

An account of all sums that have been applied to the purpose of educating the Natives in India from the year 1813 to 1830; distinguishing the Amount in each year.

	Bengal	Madras	Bombay	Total.
	£	£	£	£
1813	4,207	480	442	5,129
1814	11,606	480	499	12,585
1815	4,405	480	537	5,422
1816	5,146	480	578	6,204
1817	5,177	480	795	6,452
1818	5,211	480	630	6,321
1819	7,191	480	1,270	8,941
1820	5,807	480	1,401	7,688
1821	6,882	480	594	7,956
1822	9,081	480	594	10,155
1823	6,134	480	594	7,208
1824	19,970	480	1,434	21,884
1825	57,122	480	8,961	66,563
1826	21,623	480	5,309	27,412
1827	30,077	2,140	13,096	45,313
1828	22,797	2,980	10,064	35,841
1829	24,663	3,614	9,799	38,076
1830	28,748	2,946	12,636	44,330

* Page 483 of Appendix (L) to Report from Select Committee on the affairs of the East India Company, Vol. I. (Public).

"The following Statement exhibits the estimated Amount of the Sums annually chargeable on the Revenues of India for the support of Native Schools, as the same appear upon the Books of Establishments, and by the proceedings of the respective Governments last received from India.

I.—Bengal.

		Rs.
Calcutta	Madrissa, per annum	30,000
,,	Hindoo Sanskrit College (in which those of Nuddea and Tirhoot have merged)	25,000
,,	School Book Society	6,000
,,	School Society	6,000
,,	At the disposal of the Committee of Public Instruction (inclusive of the Chinsurah, Rajpootana and of the salary to their Secretary Rs. 6,000)	1,06,000
*,,	Old Charity Schools as rent for the court-house, per month Rs. 800	9,600
†,,	Free School	720
Benares	Sanskrit College	20,000
,,	Charity School	3,000
Cawnpore	Free School	4,800

* Both these Schools were for the benefit of Europeans and Anglo-Indians.

† Pages 433-34 of Appendix to Report from Select Committee on the affairs of the East India Company, Vol. I. (Public).

Hidgelee Madrissa	365
Moorshedabad College and School ..	16,537
TOTAL ..	2,28,022

II.—FORT ST. GEORGE.

Tanjore Schools, per annum	4,620
Sunday School at the Mount	1,200
Committee of Public Instruction for the Madras School-book Society and the collectorate and tehsildary schools ..	48,000
TOTAL ..	53,820

III.—BOMBAY.

	Rs.
Bombay School	3,600
Society for promoting the Education of the Poor within the Government of Bombay	11,385
Bombay Native School-book and School Society	12,720
Native School Society, Southern Concern ..	500
For the Education of natives on Captain Sutherland's plan	4,800
Dukshina, in the Deccan	50,000
College at Poona	15,250
The Engineer Institution at Bombay ..	180
For an English class	960
TOTAL ..	99,395

EAST INDIA HOUSE, (Sd.) THOMAS FISHER,
February 7th, 1827. *Searcher of the Records.*

Thus it would be observed that the Indian Government had to spend every year more money on the education of their civil servants, who in the three presidencies seldom exceeded more than 100 in number, than on the education of their Indian subjects, who at the lowest computation must have exceeded fifty millions of human beings.

Even the sum of one lac of rupees was not devoted to the purpose for which it was intended till the year 1823, when a Committee of Public Instruction was appointed by the Government of India, consisting of the principal functionaries at Calcutta, and the arrears of this lac of rupees from the year 1821 were accounted to this Commmittee. Mr. C. H. Cameron, in his Examination before the Select Committee of the House of Lords on the Government of Indian Territories in 1853, was asked by Lord Monteagle of Brandon on the 7th July, 1853 :—

"When you were at the head of the Council of Public Instruction, did you ever endeavour to obtain the payment of any portion of the arrears of that lac of rupees which had been left unpaid for so many years?"

His answer was, "No, we never did."

II. Private Enterprise.

It has been said before that the Government of India did not devote the sum of one lac of rupees a year to the purpose for which it had been intended by the Legislature to be spent. They did not establish any school or college for the instruction of Indians.* The Court of Directors also did not encourage the Government of India to do anything for the diffusion of education among the inhabitants of this country. In their letter to the Governor-General in Council of Bengal, dated 3rd June, 1814, the Court of Directors wrote :

"The Clause presents two distinct propositions for consideration; first, the encouragement of the learned natives of India, and the revival and improvement of literature; secondly, the promotion of a knowledge of the sciences amongst the inhabitants of that country.

"Neither of these objects is, we apprehend, to be obtained through the medium of public colleges, if established under the rules, and upon a plan similar to those that have been founded at our Universities, because the natives of caste and of reputation will not submit to the subordination and discipline of a college; and we doubt whether it would be practicable to devise any specific plan which would promise the successful accomplishment of the objects under consideration."

So the Indian Government did not take the

* The Marquess of Hastings was Governor-General of India when the Charter of the East India Company was renewed in 1813. Although he did not do much for the spread of education, his wife, Lady Hastings, established a school in Barrackpore, and under her patronage got treatises compiled for the use of the scholars.

initiative in the matter of the education of the people of this country. It was the people themselves who had to take the initiative and to do the needful. In this direction the people of Bengal were the first to understand the necessity of educating their countrymen by their own efforts. There was one man amongst them, who may be truly called the prophet of his race, who, understanding the importance of education in elevating his countrymen in the scale of nations, spared neither trouble nor money to get that object accomplished. That man was the celebrated Ram Mohun Roy. It was he who conceived the idea of that educational institution which came to be the well-known Hindoo College of Bengal. It was the first institution of its kind in India and it worked wonders, because the educated men it turned out were the pioneers of all those movements in Bengal which made that province the "Brain of India."

Although Raja Ram Mohun Roy conceived the idea of the establishment of the Hindoo College, it was Sir Edward Hyde East who was principally instrumental in establishing that institution. Sir Edward Hyde East was Chief Justice in the Supreme Court at Calcutta. In letters written to his friend Mr. Harrington, who was the senior judge of the Sudder Dewany and

Nizamat Adawlut at Calcutta, then absent in England, Sir Edward Hyde East gave an account of the origin of the Hindoo College. Extracts from these letters were published in one of the Parliamentary Blue Books,* from which the following passages are reproduced :—

In his letter, dated Calcutta, 18th May, 1816, Sir Edward Hyde East wrote:—

"An interesting and curious scene has lately been exhibited here, which shows that all things pass under change in due season. About the beginning of May a Brahmin of Calcutta,* whom I knew, and who is well-known for his intelligence and active interference among the principal native inhabitants, and also intimate with many of our own gentlemen of distinction, called upon me and informed me, that many of the leading Hindoos were desirous of forming an establishment for the education of their children in a liberal manner as practised by Europeans of condition; and desire that I would lend them my aid towards it, by having a meeting held under my sanction. Wishing to be satisfied how the Government would view such a measure, I did not at first give him a decided answer; but stated, that however much I wished well, as an individual, to such an object, yet, in the public situation I held, I should be cautious not to give any appearance of acting from my own inpulse in a matter which I

* Lords Committee's Second Report on Indian Territories, Session 1852-53, p. 235 *et seq.*

* This of course refers to Raja Ram Mohun Roy.

was sure that the Government would rather leave to them (the Hindoos) to act in, as they thought right than in any manner to control them; but that I would consider of the matter, and if I saw no objection ultimately to the course he proposed, I would inform him of it; and if he would then give me a written list of the principal Hindoos to whom he alluded, I would send them an invitation to meet at my house.

* * * *

"After his departure, I communicated to the Governor-General what had passed, who laid my communication before the Supreme Council, all the members of which approved of the course I had taken, and signified, through his Lordship, that they saw no objection to my permitting the parties to meet at my house.

"It seemed indeed to be as good an opportunity as any which could occur of feeling the general pulse of the Hindoos, as to the projected system of national moral improvement of them recommended by Parliament (and towards which they directed a lac to be annually laid out), and this without committing the Government in the experiment. The success of it has much surpassed any previous expectation. The meeting was accordingly held at my house on the 14th of May, 1816, at which 50 and upwards of the most respectable Hindoo inhabitants of rank or wealth attended, including also the principal Pundits; when a sum of nearly half-a lac of rupees was subscribed, and many more subscriptions were promised. Those who were well acquainted with this people, and know how hardly a Hindoo parts with his money upon any abstract speculation of mental advantage, will best know how to estimate this effort of theirs. It is, however, a beginning made towards improvement which surprises those who have known them the longest, and many of themselves also. Most of them, however, appeared to take great interest in the proceedings, and all expressed themselves in favour of making the acquisition of the English language a principal object of education, together with its moral and scientific productions.

"I first received some of the principal Hindoos in a room adjoining to that where the generality were to assemble. There the Pundits, to most of whom I was before unknown, were introduced to me. The usual mode of salutation was on this occasion departed from; instead of holding out money in his hand for me to touch (a base and degraded custom), the chief Pundit held out both his hands closed towards me; and as I offered him my hand, thinking he wished to shake hands in our English style, he disclosed a number of small sweet-scented flowers, which he emptied into my hand, saying that those were the flowers of literature, which they were happy to present to me on this occasion, and requested me to accept from them (adding some personal compliments). Having brought the flowers to my face, I told him that the sweet scent was an assurance to me that they would prove to be the flowers of morality, as well as of literature, to his nation, by the assistance of himself and his friends. This appeared to gratify them very much."

Ram Mohun Roy was the prime mover for

the establishment of the Hindoo College. But the leading Hindoos of Calcutta strongly objected to associate with him in this educational movement. The principal ground of their objection has been very clearly set forth by Sir Hyde East in the letter under reference. Ram Mohun Roy appeared to the Hindoos to all intents and purposes a Mussalman.

"Talking afterwards with several of the company, before I proceeded to open the business of the day, I found that one of them in particular, a Brahman of good caste, and a man of wealth and influence, was mostly set against Ram Mohun Roy, * * * * He expressed a hope that no subscription would be received from Ram Mohun Roy. I asked, why not? 'Because he has chosen to separate himself from us, and to attack our religion.' * * * *

"Upon another occasion I had asked a very sensible Brahmin what it was that made some of his people so violent against Ram Mohun. He said in truth, they did not like a man of his consequence to take open part against them; that he himself had advised Ram Mohun against it; he had told him that if he found any thing wrong among his countrymen, he should have endeavoured, by private advice and persuasion to amend it; but that the course he had taken set everybody against him, and would do no good in the end. They particularly disliked (and this I believe is at the bottom of the resentment) his associating himself so much as he does with Mussalmans, not with this or that Mussalman, as a personal friend, but being continually surrounded by them, and suspected to partake of meals with them. In fact, he has, I believe, newly withdrawn himself from the society of his brother Hindoos, whom he looked down upon, which wounds their pride.

* * * *

"The principal objects proposed for the adoption of the meeting * * were the cultivation of the Bengalee and English languages in particular; next, the Hindoostanee tongue, as convenient in the Upper Provinces; and then the Persian, if desired, as ornamental; general duty to God; the English system of morals * *; Grammar, writing (in English as well as Bengalee), Arithmetic (this is one of the Hindoo virtues), History, Geography, Astronomy, Mathematics; and in time, as the fund increases, English belles-letters, poetry, &c., &c.

"One of the singularities of the meeting was, that it was composed of persons of various castes, all combining for such a purpose, whom nothing else could have brought together; whose children are to be taught, though not fed, together.

"Another singularity was that the most distinguished Pundits who attended declared their warm approbation of all the objects proposed; and when they were about to depart the head Pundit, in the name of himself and the others, said that they rejoiced in having lived to see the day when literature (many parts of which had formerly been cultivated in their country with considerable success but which were now nearly extinct) was about to be revived with greater lustre and prospect of success than ever.

"Another meeting was proposed to be held at the distance of a week; and during this interval I continued to receive numerous applications for permission to attend it. I heard from all quarters of the approbation of the Hindoos at large to the plan; they have promised that a lac shall be subscribed to begin with. It is proposed to desire them to appoint a committee of their own for management, taking care only to secure the attendance of two or three respectable European gentlemen to aid them, and see that all goes on rightly."

It is not necessary to proceed any further with the history of this institution and its successful career. For nearly 40 years it maintained its independent existence and it turned out such scholars and workers as the late Revd. K. M. Banerji, Michael M. S. Dutt, Raja Rajendra Lala Mitra, Ram Gopal Ghose, the poet Kashi Prasad Ghose and many others whose names have become almost household words in Bengal. It was about 1854 that this institution was incorporated in what is now known as the Presidency College of Bengal. In August 1853, Dr. Frederick John Mouat, Secretary to the Council of Education, Bengal, drew up a history of the Hindoo College which was published among the selections from the

Records of the Bengal Government.* Those who are interested in the subject of education may consult this publication with profit, because it contains much valuable information.

Owing to the prejudice of his countrymen against him, Raja Ram Mohun Roy, with characteristic self-effacement, chose to sever his connection with the Hindoo College. But he never ceased to take interest in matters educational. A writer in the "Indian Echo" for 1853—presumably Mr. K. M. Chatterjee, Barrister-at-Law, a grandson of Ram Mohun Roy, wrote :—

> "It is known to but a few of our generation that Ram Mohun Roy, baffled in his objects with the Government of the day, established a school of his own, supported entirely by himself, near Cornwallis Square, which afterwards went by the name of Purna Mittra's School. In 1830, the Raja, on the eve of his departure for England, and scarcely sanguine of the success of his own institution, did all in his power to induce people to join the Free Church Institution just founded by the celebrated Dr. Duff."

As regards diffusion of education, the people of Bombay were not idle. Mr. Warden, the President of the Board of Education at Bombay, in his Report for 1853, wrote:—

> "The Board of Education, which now superintends

* No. XIV. Papers relating to the Establishment of the Presidency College of Bengal, 1854.

under the general orders of the Government, the administration of public instruction throughout the Presidency of Bombay, had its rise as follows:—

"In the year 1820, a Committee of the 'Bombay Education Society' * * formed a committee which was called 'The Native School-book and School-Committee.'"

"The main object of this Committee was to prepare and provide suitable books of instruction for the use of Native schools in the different vernacular languages and to establish and improve Native Schools; and two years later this Committee became a separate society, denominated. 'The Bombay Native School-book and School-Society.' It was for some time supported solely by voluntary subscriptions; but an appeal was made to Government for assistance, and in 1824, Government granted an annual allowance of about 6,000 rupees. In 1825, the Society purchased the ground on which the ElphinstoneCollege stands, and the name of the Society was changed to that of 'Bombay Native Education Society.'

"For several years these Societies laboured under pecuniary and other difficulties, but on the retirement of the Honourable Mountstuart Elphinstone from the Government of this Presidency in 1827, a powerful stimulus was given to the cause of education. In honour of that illustrious man, * * who had governed Bombay seven years, influential natives in every province on this side of India came forward and raised, in conjunction with Europeans, a durable monument to his memory, in the shape of a subscription to the astonishing amount of nearly £30,000, appropriated to the promotion of Native Education, * *. This liberal conduct at once placed the cause on a firm basis. It was determined to appropriate the sum raised to the foundation of 'Elphinstone Professorships,' for teaching the English language, and the arts, the sciences, and the literature of Europe. Government then came forward and placed an annual sum of 44,000 rupees at the disposal of the Directors of Education, in support of the Elphinstone Professorships, and for the use of the institutions at the Presidency.

"In 1832, a plan for the establishment of the Elphinstone Professorships was arranged. The Elphinstone College was erected, and a College Council appointed, * *. The connexion of this Society with the Elphinstone College then ceased. The management of the College, vested in the Council, became subject to the general control of Government."*

Private enterprise in the matter of education was not limited to the presidency towns of Calcutta and Bombay only, it extended also to many a mofussil station of note. Thus one Bengali gentleman named Joynarain Ghoshal, an inhabitant of Benares, presented a petition to the Marquess Hastings when his Lordship visited the Upper Provinces in 1814,

"with proposals for establishing a school in the neighbourhood of that city, and requesting that government would receive in deposit the sum of Rs. 20,000, the

* Pp : 377-78. L. Committee's Second Report on Indian Territories, 1853."

legal interest of which, together with the revenue arising from certain lands, he wished to be appropriated to the expense of the institution. The design meeting with the approbation of Government, Joynarrain Ghossal was acquainted therewith. Accordingly in July, 1818, he founded his school, appointing to the management thereof, the Rev. D. Corrie, corresponding member of the Calcutta Church Missionary Society, * * Owing to some litigation respecting the lands, with the revenues of which it was Joynarrain Ghossal's original intention to endow the school, he delivered up to Mr. Corrie a house in Benares, to be used as a school-house, and assigned a monthly revenue of 200 rupees for the support of the institution.

"Nearly 200 children, Hindoo and Mussalman, were soon collected for instruction, and great numbers continuing to apply for admission, a statement of the school was submitted, through the agents at Benares, to the Governor-General-in-Council, with an application for pecuniary aid from Government; this was immediately granted to the extent of Rs. 252-12 as. per mensem or per annum, Rs. 3,033.

"In this school, the English, Persian, Hindoostanee and Bengallee languages are taught; a number of poor children are admitted into the house, where they are subsisted and clothed; other poor children receive small allowances for subsistence out of the house. The children are admitted without regard to caste or country: no scholar is admitted under seven years of age, nor do any receive pecuniary support for more than seven years; * * A library and museum, in connection with the school, were proposed to be formed by voluntary contribution. * * * *

"In April, 1825, Colly Shunker Ghossal, son of Joynarrain Ghossal, augmented the funds of the school by a donation of Rs. 20,000. * * * *

The College at Agra was established from the rent of certain lands held by one Gungadhar Sastri.

"It is stated that in the year 1802, the local agents in the Agra District reported the existence of certain lands held by the late Gungadhar Pandit in Agra and Ally Gurh, yielding an annual rent of nearly 16,000 rupees, which constituted an endowment applicable to the maintenance of schools and seminaries of learning. The accumulated proceeds of these lands amounted to nearly 1,50,000 rupees, interest upon which being allowed, an annual income would be yielded by the endowment, of 20,000 rupees, forming a fund adequate to the support of the collegiate establishment—a scale creditable to the Government and beneficial to the people."†

In the districts of the Bombay Presidency also, several institutions for the education of the natives were founded by the voluntary contributions and donations of the people themselves. The most noteworthy of these institutions was the Native School Society of the Southern Concan.

---

* Pp: 404-405 of Appendix to Report from Select Committee on the affairs of the East India Company, Vol. I. (Public).

† *Ibid*, p. 408.

"This Society was formed on the 15th June, 1823, by the exertions of Lieutenant J. B. Jervis, for the establishment of native schools in the Southern Concan. It commenced its operations with a fund amounting, in annual subscriptions and donations, to 1,600 rupees, including some liberal contributions made by natives of distinction. With this sum three schools were established at Rutnagherry, Nandwera, and Chiploon, for instruction in the Mahratta language. * * * *

"Material assistance in the establishment and management of these schools appears to have been derived from two public-spirited natives, Mahomed Ibrahim Pacha and Vittoba Ragoonath Caunt, * * *"*

Patcheappah's Schools.

Although these schools in the Madras Presidency were not established during the period of which we are treating here, yet this seems to be the proper place to refer to them. Regarding these schools, it is stated in an official publication:—

"The founding of Patcheappah's Schools marks indeed an era in the history of Madras education, as it was the first example of intelligent natives of various castes combining to aid the cause of popular instruction. Patcheappah, in whose name these institutions are founded, was a wealthy Hindoo, who, dying in the last (18th) century, left one lakh of pagodas by his

* *Ibid*, pp. 430-31.

will for the establishment of charities, chiefly of a religious character, but in part dedicated to objects of general benevolence. The Advocate-General, Sir Herbert Compton, having discovered that these charities were totally unperformed, and the funds spoliated by the successive executors of his will, filed an information in the Supreme Court, and obtained a general decree against the party finally liable for an account of the fund, to be paid with accumulated interest—amounting to many lakhs of rupees—and also for the performance of the charities. In the whole there were finally collected to the credit of the charities nearly eight lakhs of rupees. A scheme was prepared, whereby, in due accordance with the provisions of the will, and without trenching upon any specific religious or benevolent charities mentioned in the will, it was proposed that all the accumulated sums beyond one lakh of pagodas (that is, upwards of four lakhs of rupees with all accumulating interest) should be devoted to educational establishments in various parts of the Presidency, and particularly at Madras. The scheme provided all details for the quality, localities, subjects of instruction, and governance of these institutions; and they were all finally incorporated in a decree of the Court. After some years directions were given, under Lord Elphinstone's government, for the Board of Revenue making such orders as were necessary to carry out the decree of the Supreme Court and the wishes of the Court of Directors. A school in Black Town was established in January, 1842, for affording gratuitous education to the poorer classes of the native community in the elemenary branches of English literature and science, coupled with instruction in Tameel and Telegoo. * * * * * In the same year [1846] the Patcheappah trustees took over the charities of another rich native named Govindoo Naidoo. In 1856, scholarships were given in this benefactor's name at Patcheappah's Schools, and later on a separate Primary School was opened from the same funds. The new institution was called "Govindoo Naidoo's Primary School," and was opened in 1864. In the year 1869 a third school of equal importance was established by means of a bequest from C. Sreenivassa Pillay, who had been for several years president of Patcheappah's charities."

[P. 570, Vol. I, Madras Manual of Administration.]

It is not necessary to multiply other instances of private enterprise in matters educational between the years 1813—1833. In the light of the facts narrated here, it cannot be said that the Government took the initiative in the diffusion of education or rather high education amongst the people of India. Heaven helps those who help themselves. And it was because the people tried to help themselves in education that the educational policy of Government met with some amount of success. The British mode of the administration of India reduced the people to rank poverty and made them quite helpless and hence they were unable to be quite independent of State aid in education.

EDUCATION OF INDIANS (1833—1853).

(*Anglicisation of Education*).

In the Charter Act of 1833 no clause expressive of motives of philanthropy and altruism in promoting the happiness and interest of the natives of India was inserted. But the grant of one lac in 1813 had to be increased now tenfold, for by 1833 a much larger portion of the map of India was dyed red than had been the case twenty years earlier. The Indian Government, however, did not take the lead in founding colleges and schools for the diffusion of education among their subjects. But what they did within two years of the passing of the Charter Act was the anglicisation of education. The controversy between the two schools known as occidentalists and orientalists came to a close in 1835 when the then Governor-General of India, Lord Bentinck, issued his famous minute by which he anglicised the educational system of India.

It is necessary here to say something about the origin and history of the controversy between the orientalists and occidentalists. In Bengal, when the Committee of Public Instruction was formed in 1823, Horace Hayman Wilson was appointed its Secretary. Although he came out to India in the capacity of a medical officer in the service of the Company, he did not practise his profession in this country, but devoted his attention to the study of Indian philology, antiquities and ethnology. He was a renowned Sanskrit scholar. But like other Anglo-Indians of his class, he looked upon India as the happy hunting ground for his correligionists and compatriots and therefore tried to keep its inhabitants in bondage and perpetual tutelage of England. It was this motive which prompted him to be an advocate of the cause of oriental learning and not to teach Indians English. On this point he expressed himself so clearly in his evidence before the Select Committee of the House of Lords on the Government of Indian Territories on the 5th July, 1853, that a portion of it is reproduced below. He did not want Indians in the covenanted ranks of the Indian Medical Service. For in his evidence he said:—

"In truth, it would be difficult to render the services of Native medical attendants acceptable to the Europeans, as there is a great feeling of dislike to them. Europeans in India cannot be made to believe that Native Surgeons are fully qualified, although no doubt many of them are very efficient even, as we know; for we have had two or three of them over in this country, and one of them particularly was very highly distinguished in the medical classes; he took his degree both at the College of Physicians and the College of Surgeons, Dr. Chuckerbutty; but still you cannot get over the prejudice which Europeans entertain against them, and that is not the direction in which their services are most valuable."

In plain language he meant to say that Indians should not be admitted to the ranks of the Indian Medical Service, because the Europeans entertained prejudice against them! He was asked by Lord Boughton:

"7279. Do you know that an effort was made to induce the East India Company to employ one or two of those Native medical students in their own medical service?"

In reply to which, H. H. Wilson said:—

"I have heard so; I do not know it; I do not think it is necessary."

He was further asked by Lord Boughton:—

"7280. Particularly that individual whom you mentioned just now?

"Yes; I have heard that some of his friends think that he has been rather ungenerously treated in not being appointed to the Company's Service.

"7281. Do you see any objection to the employment occasionally of very eminent medical students in the covenanted service?

"You have to encounter a very strong feeling on the part of all European society against it.

"7282. But if the Europeans did not choose to employ those persons in the medical profession, of course they would not be obliged to employ them?

"At a civil station very often they would have no choice. There is but one medical man attached to a station; and if he were a Native officer, whatever his qualifications might be, I am sure there would be a very strong feeling against employing him; it would be very repugnant to the prejudices of Europeans; I do not think the benefit of either the country or of the individual would be consulted by forcing him into that position in which he could not be of so much use to his countrymen as he might be in independent practice, and in which he would find himself in an uncomfortable position; the other medical officers of the Company would always be inclined to look with jealousy and dislike upon him.

* * * *

"7284. Would it not give additional reputation to the Native medical practitioners if they were occasionally employed in the Company's Service?

"* * I do not think that any advantage would result from incorporating even qualified Natives in the Company's Medical Service."

He was also against establishing universities in India on the plan of English ones for the following reasons. He said:—

"I do not know what is meant by a university in India; if it is to consist in wearing caps and gowns, and being called Bachelors of Arts and Masters of Arts, I do not see what advantage is likely to accrue from it. The Natives certainly could not appreciate the value of such titles, it would be of no advantage to a young man to be called a Bachelor of Arts amongst Natives of India, who could attach no positive idea to it; *it would be inconvenient if it gave him place and precedence amongst Europeans;* in fact I cannot consider that any advantages at all would be derived from such an institution."

It is not difficult therefore to understand the motives which prompted Wilson to take his stand against English education. He did not want Indians to stand on the same level with his countrymen. If they were educated in English, then it would be inconvenient for Anglo-Indians to treat Indians with that supreme contempt which was their wont in their dealings with the latter.

It can be safely asserted that the same feelings guided the conduct of other orientalists like Shakespeare and the Prinsep brothers.

But at that time was living a Bengali who thoroughly understood the temperament of those 'birds of passage' in India who in order to keep Indians in bondage were averse to giving them English education. That Bengali was the celebrated Raja Ram Mohun Roy. To checkmate the machinations of the scheming and designing Anglo-Indian Orientalists, he addressed in December. 1823, a letter to the then Governor-General of

India, Lord Amherst, extracts from which are given below:—

"We find that the Government are establishing a Sanskrit school under Hindoo Pundits to impart such knowledge as is already current in India. * *

"From these considerations, as the sum set apart for the instruction of the natives of India was intended by the Government in England for the improvement of its Indian subjects, I beg leave to state, with due deference to your Lordship's exalted situation, that if the plan now adopted be followed it will completely defeat the object proposed, since no improvement can be expected from inducing young men to consume a dozen of years of the most valuable period of their lives in acquiring the niceties of Vyakaran or Sanskrit Grammar. * *

"If it had been intended to keep the British nation in ignorance of real knowledge, the Baconian philosophy would not have been allowed to displace the system of the schoolmen, which was the best calculated to perpetuate ignorance. In the same manner, the Sanskrit system of education would be best calculated to keep this country in darkness, if such had been the policy of the British legislature. But as the improvement of the native population is the object of the Government, it will consequently promote a more liberal and enlightened system of instruction; embracing mathematics, natural philosophy, chemistry, anatomy, with other useful sciences, which may be accomplished with the sum proposed by employing a few gentlemen of talents and learning in Europe, and providing a college furnished with necessary books, instruments and other apparatus."

It is on record that—

"The Bengal Government regarded this letter as having been penned under a somewhat erroneous impression respecting the views of Government in the establishment of the Sanskrit College, but forwarded the letter to the Committee of Public Instruction for their information."*

The controversy then was set afoot by Ram Mohun Roy, and the members of the Education Commission appointed by Lord Ripon in 1882 in the sixth chapter of their report, referring to Ram Mohun Roy's exertions, wrote:—

"It took twelve years of controversy, the advocacy of Macaulay, and the decisive action of a new Governor-General, before the Committee could, as a body, acquiesce in the policy urged by him."

The Court of Directors in their letter to the Governor-General in Council of Bengal, dated 18th January, 1824, wrote:—

"With respect to the sciences, it is worse than a waste of time to employ persons either to teach or to learn them in the state in which they are found in the Oriental books. As far as any historical documents may be found in the Oriental languages, what is desirable is, that they should be translated, and this, it is

* Appendix to Report from Select Committee on the Affairs of the East India Company, Vol. I. (Public), p. 436.

evident, will best be accomplished by Europeans who have acquired the requisite knowledge. Beyond these branches what remains in Oriental literature is poetry; but it has never been thought necessary to establish colleges for the cultivation of poetry, nor is it certain that this would be the most effectual expedient for the attainment of the end.

" In the meantime we wish you to be fully apprised of our zeal for the progress and improvement of education among the natives of India, and of our willingness to make considerable sacrifices to that important end, if proper means for the attainment of it could be pointed out to us. But we apprehend that the plan of the institutions, to the improvement of which our attention is now directed, was originally and fundamentally erroneous. The great end should not have been to teach Hindoo learning but useful learning. No doubt, in teaching useful learning to the Hindoos or Mahomedans, Hindoo Media or Mahomedan Media, as far as they were found most effectual, would have been proper to be employed, and Hindoo and Mahomedan prejudices would have needed to be consulted, while everything which was useful in Hindoo or Mahomedan literature, it would have been proper to retain; nor would there have been any insuperable difficulty in introducing under these reservations a system of instruction from which great advantage might have been derived. In professing on the other hand to establish seminaries for the purpose of teaching mere Hindoo or mere Mahomedan literature, you bound yourselves to teach a great deal of what was frivolous, not a little of what was purely mischievous, and a small remainder indeed in which utility was in any way concerned."*

"The Bengal Government, on receipt of the Court's letter, communicated it to the Committee of General Instruction, who in reply submitted some observations in vindication of this establishment as it then existed.

"Admitting that the legitimate object to be pursued was the introduction of European science to the extinction of that which is falsely so called by Hindoos and Mahomedans, circumstances, it was observed, had rendered necessary the course which had been pursued, and it was questionable 'whether the Government could originally have founded any other seminaries than those which it actually had established, *viz.*, the Madrissa, to teach Mahomedan literature and law, and the Benares College, to teach Sanskrit Literature and Hindoo law. The absence of all media, either teachers or books, for instruction of a different kind, the necessity for which has been acknowledged by the Court of Directors, was considered fully to have justified the course which had been pursued.

"It was further observed, as justifying that course, that the Government stood pledged to its adoption, in the case of the 'Sanscrit College in Calcutta, which was substituted for two colleges proposed to be endowed at Tirhoot and Nuddea, the original object of which was declaredly the preservation and encouragement of Hindoo learning; that the state of public feeling in

* *Ibid*, p. 488. It is believed that this letter was written by Mr. James Mill, the historian and father of John Stuart Mill, the philosopher. Mr. Mill occupied an important position in the India Office.

India did not then appear to warrant any general introduction of Western literature and science, although the prejudices of the natives against European interference with their education in any shape had considerably abated; that the substitution of European for native superintendence over all the schools maintained by Government was an important change which had been effected, and from the continuance of which exercised with temper and discretion, it was expected that the confidence of the officers and pupils of the several seminaries would be won to an extent that would pave the way for the unopposed introduction of such improvements as the Government might thereafter have the means of effecting; and finally, that a necessity still existed for the creation of those media by which useful science was to be diffused, that is, by teaching native teachers and providing books in the languages of India.

"On the unfavourable view taken by the Court of the state of science among the natives of India, the committee remarked as follows :—

"The position, that it is worse than a waste of time to employ persons either to teach or learn the sciences in the state in which they are found in oriental books, 'is of so comprehensive a nature, that it obviously requires considerable modification, and the different branches of science intended to be included in it, must be particularized before a correct appreciation can be formed of their absolute and comparative value. The metaphysical sciences, as found in Sanscrit and Arabic writings, are, we believe, fully as worthy of being studied in those languages as in any other. The

Arithmetic and Algebra of the Hindoos lead to the same result and are grounded on the same principles as those of Europe: and in the Madrissa, the Elements of Mathematical science which are taught are those of Euclid. Law, a principal object of study in all the institutions, is one of vital importance to the good government of the country, and language is the ground work upon which all future improvements must materially depend. To diffuse a knowledge of those things, language and law specially, cannot therefore be considered a waste of time.'

"The Committee conclude their letter by observing, on the subjects of history and poetry, that the attachment of the Mahomedans to their own history is great; that no good reason appeared why the natives of India should be debarred from cultivating their own historical records, or why the transactions of the country in which they had a natural interest should not be thought deserving of their persual; and that poetry was a branch of study in all colleges, having ever been found to be a valuable auxiliary in the study of literature in every language and country. 'As a part therefore, and a very important part of Sanskrit and Arabic literature, as the source of national imagery, the expression of national feeling, and the depositary of the most approved phraseology and style, the poetical writings of the Hindoos and Mohamedans appear to be legitimately comprehended amongst the objects of literary seminaries founded for Mahomedans and Hindoos."*

* *Ibid*, pp. 436-437.

It cannot be denied that there was much force and reason in the above arguments. But the Education Committee did nothing for the cultivation of the vernaculars. They were content with encouraging the learning of Sanskrit and Arabic, and all that was contained in the literatures of those two classical languages. But they neglected to instruct the students under their supervision in the sciences and arts of Europe. Had they done that, there would not have been any case for the occidentalists at all.

But the cause of the occidentalists received much impetus from the appointment of Lord Bentinck as Governor-General of India. Bentinck had been at one time Governor of Madras and was mainly responsible for the Mutiny at Vellore. He was, therefore, disgraced and recalled from the Governorship of that Presidency. It was not out of love for Indians but from motives of political expediency that he wanted their anglicisation. He thought that would perhaps strengthen the hold of England on India.*

---

* Sir Charles Trevelyan—brother-in-law of Macaulay—who was also a tower of strength to the occidentalists, in his evidence on 23rd June, 1853 before the Select Committee of the House of Lords on the Government of Indian Territories, said :—

"According to the unmitigated native system, the Mahomedans regard us as *kafirs*, as infidel usurpers of some of the finest realms of Islam, for it is a tenet of that dominant and warlike religion constantly to strive for political supremacy, and to hold all other races in subjection. According to the

It should be mentioned here that Bentinck was not in favour of educating Indians.

He saw danger in the spread of knowledge in this country. So he recorded his opinion in a Minute, dated the 13th March, 1835. Sir Charles

---

same original native views, the Hindoos regard us as *mlechhas*, that is, impure outcasts, with whom no communion ought to be held; and they all of them, both Hindoo and Mahomedan, regard us as usurping foreigners, who have taken their country from them, and exclude them from the avenues to wealth and distinction. The effect of a training in European learning is to give an entirely new turn to the native mind. The young men educated in this way cease to strive after independence according to the original Native model, and aim at improving the institutions of the country according to the English model, with the ultimate result of establishing constitutional self-government. They cease to regard us as enemies and usurpers, and they look upon us as friends and patrons, and powerful beneficent persons, under whose protection all they have most at heart for the regeneration of their country will gradually be worked out. According to the original native view of political change, we might be swept off the face of India in a day, and, as a matter of fact, those who look for the improvement of India according to this model are continually meditating on plots and conspiracies with that object; whereas, according to the new and improved system, the object must be worked out by very gradual steps, and ages may elapse before the ultimate end will be attained, and in the meantime the minority, who already regard us with respect, and aim at regenerating their country with our assistance, will receive continual accessions, until in the course of time they become the majority; but when that will be, no one can say; nor can any one say how long we may continue to be politically connected with India even after the whole of the civil employments have been transferred to the natives. If we take the proper course, there may be an intermediate period similar to that at which we are arrived with respect to Canada and Australia. Supposing our connexion with India to cease according to the native views, it will cease suddenly—it will cease by a violent convulsion—it will cease with most irritated feelings on both sides, and we shall leave a hostile country, and a country which will be to a great extent unimproved. Whereas if the connexion ceases according to the other course of circumstances, we shall leave a grateful country and a highly improved country."

Metcalfe, after he had assumed the Governor-Generalship of India, in a Minute, dated the 16th May, 1835, said :

"His Lordship (Bentinck), however, sees further danger in the spread of knowledge and the operations of the Press. I do not, for my own part, anticipate danger as a certain consequence from these causes. I see so much danger in the ignorance, fanaticism, and barbarism of our subjects, that I rest on the spread of knowledge some hope of greater strength and security. Men will be better able to appreciate the good and evil of our rule; and if the good predominate, they will know that they may lose by a change. Without reckoning on the affection of any, it seems probable that those of the natives who would most deprecate and least promote our overthrow, would be the best-informed and most enlightened among them, unless they had themselves, individually, ambitious dreams of power.

Then he was asked by Lord Monteagle of Brandon, "For a very long time, as long as the educated classes of India are a small minority in a country, with the enormous population of India, must it not necessarily be the fact that the educated classes must, for their own sakes, be more in association with English interests than they can be with any system of Hindoo advancement, as separate from the English interests?"

In reply to the above question, Sir Charles Trevelyan said:—

"For a long time to come it would be greatly to their disadvantage that a Native Government should be established. They would be the first who would suffer from it. They would be the objects of plunder and popular indignation, and it is every way their interest to hold by us; and as that class increases, the larger will be the proportion of the people who will become attached to us."

It can not be denied that Sir Charles reflected the views, opinions and sentiments of the occidentalists, of Lord Bentinck and others who were instrumental in introducing English education in India.

If, however, the extension of knowledge is to be a new source of danger—and I will not pretend confidently to predict the contrary—it is one altogether unavoidable. It is our duty to extend knowledge whatever may be the result; and spread it would, even if we impeded it. The time is passed when the operations of the Press could be effectually restrained even if that course would be any source of safety, which must be very doubtful. Nothing so precarious could in prudence be trusted to. If, therefore, increase of danger be really to be apprehended from inorease of knowledge, it is what we must cheerfully submit to. We must not try to avert it, and if we did we should fail."*

Lord Bentinck was not in favour of educating the people of this country, but he was desirous of anglicising them or rather preventing them from forming a hom'ogeneous nation. With that object in view, the first thing which he did—the thing which he as Governor-General of India had the power to do, was the introduction of English as the court-language of India. The Court of Directors in their letter, dated 29th September, 1830, to Bengal, wrote :

ith a view to give the natives an additional motive to the acquisition of the English language, you have it in comtemplation gradually to introduce English as the language of public business in all its departments, and you have determined to begin at once by

* Kaye's Selections from the Papers of Lord Metcalfe, p. 197.

adopting the practice of corresponding in English with all native princes or persons of rank who are known to understand that language, or to have persons about them who understand it. *From the meditated change in the language of public business, including judical proceedings, you anticipate several collateral advantages, the principal of which is, that the judge, or other European officer, being thoroughly acquainted with the language in which the proceedings are held, will be, and appear to be, less dependent upon the natives by whom he is surrounded, and those natives will in consequence, enjoy fewer opportunities of bribery or other undue emolument.*"

The passage italicised above shows the real motive for unduly favouring and encouraging the English language. The interest of the millions of Indians was to be sacrificed for the convenience and profit of a handful of birds of passage in India. A very large influx of the Britishers in India was taking place, therefore, for their convenience, English was made the language of business.

English was the language of the rulers; so the thoughtful portion of the Indian community were doing their best to learn it themselves and teach it to their children. Thus regarding the Calcutta Hindoo College, the Court of Directors in their letter of 29th September, 1830, an extract from which has been given above, wrote :

"But the Vidyalaya or Anglo-Indian College, originally established by the natives themselves, for the study of the English language, and for education through the medium of that language exclusively, has had more decided success than either of the other Calcutta colleges. The number of scholars is now 436, of whom all except 100 pay for their tuition. The progress of these pupils is highly encouraging, the higher classes being able to compose tolerably in English, and to read the best authors in the English language.

Further on, they wrote :

"Your attention has been anxiously directed to the means of accomplishing this object, and in particular to the comparative expediency of establishing separate English Colleges, or of enlarging the plan of the existing institutions, so as to render them adequate to that more extensive purpose. You have transmitted to us several most interesting communications from the general Committee of Public Instruction, and from the local Committee of Delhi College, on this question.

"Both the committees give a decided preference to the plan of establishing separate colleges for the study of English, and for the cultivation of European knowledge through the medium of the English language. They urge that a thorough knowledge of English can only be acquired by natives through a course of study beginning early in life, and continued for many years; that the knowledge of our language and of European science which could be acquired in a course of education mainly directed to other objects, would not contribute in any high degree to the improvement of the native character and intellect, while the native languages and literature may be adequately pursued, as a subordinate branch of education, in an English college; and that anything beyond the mere elements of European science is most advantageously taught through the European languages, with the additional recommendation, that when so taught, it comes into less direct collision with the sacred books of the Mahomedans and Hindoos.

" By these arguments you have been convinced, and you have accordingly authorized the establishment of an English College at Delhi and another at Benares. The project of establishing one at Calcutta seems to have been tacitly abandoned; the Anglo-Indian College, under its present superintendence, being found capable of answering the purpose.

" While we attach much more importance than is attached by the two committees, to the amount of useful instruction which can be communicated to the natives through their own languages, we fully concur with them in thinking it highly advisable to enable and encourage a large number of natives to acquire a thorough knowledge of English; being convinced that the higher tone and better spirit of European literature con produce their full effect only on those who become familiar with them in the original languages. While, too, we agree with the committee that the higher branches of science may be more advantageously studied in the languages of Europe, than in translation into the oriental tongues, it is also to be considered that the fittest persons for translating English scientific books, or for putting their substance into a shape adapted to Asiatic students, are natives who have studied profoundly in the original works.

"On these grounds we concur with you in thinking it desirable that the English course of education should be kept separate from the course of oriental study at the native colleges, and should be attended for the most part by a different set of students."

The recommendations and suggestions of the Court of Directors were very fair and had they been acted upon by the Indian Government, there would have been hope for the growth of the vernaclar literatures of India. But it was selfish considerations which prompted the majority of Anglo-Indians to strive to make English the medium of instruction. Thus Mountstuart Elphinstone, the Governor of Bombay, in a Minute, dated 13th December, 1823, wrote :

"If English could be at all diffused among persons who have the least time for reflection, the progress of knowledge, by means of it, would be accelerated in a tenfold ratio, since every man who made himself acquainted with a science through the English, would be able to communicate it, in his own language, to his countrymen. At present, however, there is but little desire to learn English with any such view. The first step towards creating such a desire would be to establish a school at Bombay where English might be taught classically, and where instruction might also be given in that language on history, geography and the popular branches of science. * * * *

"Should we ever be able to extend English schools to the out-stations, admittance to them might be made a reward of merit in other studies, which tend to render it an object of ambition, or, at least, to remove all suspicion of our wishing to force our own opinions on the natives.".

One of the members of the Council of the Bombay Government, Mr. F. Warden, in a Minute, dated 29th December, 1823, also wrote :

"No doubt the progress of knowledge can be most effectually and economically promoted by a study of the English language, wherein, in every branch of science, we have, ready compiled, the most useful works, which cannot be compressed in tracts and translated in the native languages without great expense and the labour of years. A classical knowledge of English ought to constitute the chief object of the Bombay seminary. As far as I have conversed with the natives they are anxious that their children should be thoroughly grounded in the English language; some of the wealthiest would be glad to send their children to England for education, were it not for the clamorous objection of their mothers; nothing can be more favourable for commencing, or for the establishment of a good system of education, than such a disposition."

In another Minute dated 24th March, 1828, Mr. F. Warden wrote :

"In the 24th para. of my Judicial Minute of the

25th of June, 1819, I alluded to the very strong desire that had sprung up amongst the natives to avail themselves of the facilities which had been afforded of acquiring the benefit of a better education. In a subsequent discussion, I noticed the eagerness the natives had displayed to obtain a knowledge of the English Language, and enlarged on that subject in my Minute of the 6th of April, 1825. * *

"I have urged the policy of directing our chief effort to one object, to a diffusion of a knowledge of the English language, as best calculated to facilitate the intellectual and moral improvement of India. We have as yet made that only a secondary object.

"I must confess that I did not expect to receive so unqualified a corroboration of the popularity at least of that opinion among the natives as is afforded by the letter from the leading members of the native community of Bombay, bringing forward a proposition for establishing professorships to be denominated the Elphinstone professorships, for the purpose of teaching the natives the English language, and the arts, sciences and literature of Europe, to be held in the first instance by learned men to be invited from Great Britain, until natives of the country shall be found perfectly competent to undertake the office.

"No did I expect to find so decisive a proof of the facility with which the English language could be diffused as is evidenced by the report recently published in the papers, of an examination at Calcutta, of the natives educated at that presidency, which exhibits a display of proficiency in that tongue almost incredible.

"Under these impressions, I subscribe entirely to

the opinion expressed by the author of the Political History of India, that it is better and safer to commence by giving a good deal of knowledge to a few than a little to many, to be satisfied with laying the foundation stone of a good edifice, and not desire to accomplish in a day what must be the work of a century.

"But the object of giving a good deal of knowledge to a few can only be promoted by a better system of education; and the surest mode of diffusing a better system is by making the study of the English language the primary, and not merely the secondary object of attention in the education of the natives. The reviewer of the work above alluded to remarks, in which I still more cordially concur, that *a more familiar and extended acquaintance with the English language* would, to the natives, be the surest source of intellectual improvement, and *might become the most durable tie between Britain and India.*

"In any plan, therefore, for the public education of the natives, the complete knowledge of our language ought to form so prominent an object as to lay ground for its gradually becoming at least the established vehicle of legal and official business. The English tongue would in India, as in Aemrica, be the lasting monument of our dominion; * * "

So it was selfishness, if not 'enlightened selfishness,' which prompted the occidentalists to advocate the cause of English education. But Mr. Warden was in favour of educating Indians in English, because it would supply men for the

State service. In his Minute of 29th December, 1823, he wrote :

> "The field for employment then appears to me to be sufficiently wide. It is our object to render it more inviting, by assigning greater salaries to natives of talent and assiduity. That India has supplied, and will continue under our government to supply, functionaries of that character, able and expert in the administration of justice, and keen and intelligent in a knowledge of revenue details, there is evidence abundant on the records of India, published and unpublished, whilst in respect to commerce, and a conversancy with accounts, *the natives display a knowledge by which Europeans profit in no ordinary degree.*"

Diffusion of English education was demanded because then by the knowledge of the natives Europeans would profit in still greater degree.

Mr. Warden's Minute reads not unlike that of Macaulay to which reference will be made presently. The fallacies underlying Mr. Warden's arguments are the same as those of Macaulay.

Sir John Malcolm, who was Governor of Bombay in 1828, was not in favour of making English the medium of instruction. In his Minute of 1828, Malcolm wrote :

> "The chief ground on which I anticipate advantages from the establishment of the Elphinstone professorships, is, that a certain proportion of the natives will be instructed by them not only in the English

language, but in every branch of useful science. To natives so educated I look for aid, in the diffusion of knowledge among their countrymen, through the medium of their vernacular dialects; and I certainly think it is only by knowledge being accessible through the latter medium that it ever can be propagated to any general or beneficial purpose."

It was from reasons of political expediency that Malcolm was averse to educate Indians in English. For he wrote,—

"I have on political grounds a consolation, derived from my conviction of the impossibility of our ever disseminating that half knowledge of our language, which is all any considerable number of natives could attain. It would decrease that positive necessity which now exists for the servants of Government making themselves masters of the languages of the countries in which they are employed, and without which they never can become in any respect competent to their public duties."

Sir Charles E. Trevelyan, K.C.B., brother-in-law of Macaulay, had himself greatly helped the cause of the Anglicists. He submitted to the Parliamentary Committee of 1853 on Indian territories a paper on "The political tendency of the different systems of education in use in India." This document is so important that copious extracts from it are reproduced below:

"A nation which made so great a sacrifice to

redeem a few hundred thousand Negroes from slavery,* would shudder at the idea of keeping a hundred millions of Indians in the bondage of ignorance, with all its frightful consequences, by means of a political system supported by the revenue taken from the Indians themselves. Whether we govern India ten or a thousand years, we will do our duty by it, we will look, not to the probable duration of our trust, but to the satisfactory discharge of it, so long as it shall please God to contnue it to us. *Happily, however, we are not on this occasion called upon to make any effort of disinterested magnanimity. Interest and duty are never really separated in the affairs of nations, any more than they are in those of individuals; and in this case they are indissolubly united, as a very slight examination will suffice to show.*

"The Arabian or Mahomedan system is based on the exercise of power and the indulgence of passion. Pride, ambition, the love of rule, and of sensual enjoyment, are called in to the aid of religion. The earth is the inheritance of the Faithful; all besides are infidel usurpers, with whom no measures are to be kept, except

---

* It was not from any motive of philanthropy that England redeemed a few hundred thousand Negroes from slavery. In a leading article on the "Armenian Problem," the London *Times* of Tuesday, September 8, 1896, wrote:—

"Foreigners disbelieve in the existence of the philanthropic ideas and feelings amongst us; they naturally believe that when we allege them as a ground of international action we are using them as a cloak to cover ulterior ends. Quite recently one of the greatest of modern German historians ascribed England's zeal against the slave trade at the Congress of Verona to her commercial jealousy. England, says Von Treitschke, had her own colonies well supplied with negroes. She protested against the slave-trade because she desired to deprive her rivals of a similar advantage."

what policy may require. Universal dominion belongs to the Mahomedans by Divine right. Their religion obliges them to establish their predominance by the sword; and those who refuse to conform are to be kept in a state of slavish subjection. The Hindoo system, although less fierce and aggressive than the Mahomedan, is still more exclusive: all who are not Hindoos are impure outcasts, fit only for the most degraded employments; and, of course, utterly disqualified for the duties of Government, which are reserved for the military, under the guidance of the priestly caste. Such is the political tendency of the Arabic and Sanskrit systems of learning. Happily for us, these principles exist in their full force only in books written in difficult languages, and in the minds of a few learned men; and they are very faintly reflected in the feelings and opinions of the body of the people. But what will be thought of that plan of national education which would revive them and make them popular; would be perpetually reminding the Mahomedans that we are infidel usurpers of some of the fairest realms of the Faithful, and the Hindoos, that we are unclean beasts, with whom it is a sin and a shame to have any friendly intercourse? Our bitterest enemies could not desire more than that we should propagate systems of learning which excite the strongest feelings of human nature against ourselves.

"The spirit of English literature, on the other hand, cannot but be favourable to the English connection. Familiarly asquainted with us by means of our literature, the Indian youth almost cease to regard us as foreigners. They speak of our great men with the same enthusiasm as we do. Educated in the same way, interested in the same objects, engaged in the same pursuits with ourselves, they become more English than Hindoos, just as the Roman provincials became more Romans than Gauls or Italians. What is it that makes us what we are, except living and conversing with English people, and imbibing English thoughts and habits of mind? They do so too: they daily converse with the best and wisest Englishmen through the medium of their works; and form, perhaps, a higher idea of our nation than if their intercourse with it were of a more personal kind. Admitted behind the scenes they become acquainted with the principles which guide our proceedings; they see how sincerely we study the benefit of India in the measures of our administration; and from violent opponents, or sullen conformists, they are converted into zealous and intelligent co-operators with us. They learn to make a proper use of the freedom of discussion which exists under our government, by observing how we use it ourselves; and they cease to think of violent remedies, because they are convinced that there is no indisposition on our part to satisfy every real want of the country. Dishonest and bad rulers alone derive any advantage from the ignorance of their subjects. As long as we study the benefit of India in our measures, the confidence and affection of the people will increase in proportion to their knowledge of us.

"But this is not all. There is a principle in human nature which impels all mankind to aim at improving their condition; every individual has his plan of happiness; every community has its ideas of securing the national honour and prosperity. This powerful and universal principle, in some shape or other, is in a state of constant activity; and if it be not enlisted on our side, it must be arrayed against us. As long as the natives are left to brood over their former independence, their sole specific for improving their condition is, the immediate and total expulsion of the English. A native patriot of the old school has no notion of anything beyond this; his attention has never been called to any other mode of restoring the dignity and prosperity of his country. It is only by the infusion of European ideas, that a new direction can be given to the national views. The young men, brought up at our seminaries, turn with contempt from the barbarous despotism under which their ancestors groaned, to the prospect of improving their national institutions on the English model. * * So far from having the idea of driving the English into the sea uppermost in their minds, they have no notion of any improvement but such as rivets their connection with the English, and makes them dependent on English protection and instruction. * *

"The existing connection between two such distant countries as England and India, cannot, in the nature of things, be permanent; no effort of policy can prevent the natives from ultimately regaining their independence. But there are two ways of arriving at this point. One of these is, through the medium of revolution; the other, through that of reform. In one, the forward movement is sudden and violent, in the other, it is gradual and peaceable. One must end in a complete alienation of mind and separation of interest between ourselves and the natives; the other in a permanent alliance, founded on mutual benefit and good will.

"The only means at our disposal for preventing the one and securing the other class of results is, to set the natives on a process of European improvement, to which they are already sufficiently inclined. They will then cease to desire and aim at independence on the old Indian footing. A sudden change will then be impossible; and a long continuance of our present connection with India will even be assured to us. * * The natives will not rise against us, because we shall stoop to raise them; there will be no reaction, because there will be no pressure; the national activity will be fully and harmlessly employed in acquiring and diffusing European knowledge, and naturalising European institutions. The educated classes, knowing that the elevation of their country on these principles can only be worked out under our protection, will naturally cling to us. They even now do so. There is no class of our subjects to whom we are so thoroughly necessary as those whose opinions have been cast in the English mould; they are spoiled for a purely native regime; they have everything to fear from the premature establishment of a native government; their education would mark them out for persecution. * * * * This class is at present a small minority, but it is continually receiving accessions from the youth who are brought up at the different English seminaries. It will in time become the majority; and it will then be necessary to modify the political institutions to suit the increased intelligence of the people, and their capacity for self-government. * *

"In following this course we should be trying no new experiment. The Romans at once civilised the nations of Europe, and attached them to their rule by Romanising them; or, in other words, by educating them in the Roman literature and arts, and teaching them to emulate their conquerors instead of opposing them. Acquisitions made by superiority in war, were consolidated by superiority in the arts of peace; and the remembrance of the original violence was lost in that of the benefits which resulted from it. The provincials of Italy, Spain, Africa and Gaul, having no ambition except to imitate the Romans, and to share their privileges with them, remained to the last faithful subjects of the Empire; and the union was at last dissolved, not by internal revolt, but the shock of external violence, which involved conquerors and conquered in one common overthrow. The Indians will, I hope, soon stand in the same position towards us in which we once stood towards the Romans. Tacitus informs us, that it was the policy of Julius Agricola to instruct the sons of the leading men among the Britons in the literature and science of Rome and to give them a taste for the refinements of Roman civilization. We all know how well this plan answered. From being obstinate enemies, the Britons soon became attached and confiding friends; and they made more strenuous efforts to retain the Romans, than their ancestors had done to resist their invasion. It will be a shame to us if, with our greatly superior advantages, we also do not make our premature departure be dreaded as a calamity.

It must not be said in after ages, that 'the groans of the Britons' were elicited by the breaking up of the Roman Empire; and the groans of the Indians by the continued existence of the British.

* * * *

"These views were not worked out by reflection, but were forced on me by actual observation and experience. I passed some years in parts of India, where owing to the comparative novelty of our rule and to the absence of any attempt to alter the current of native feeling, the national habits of thinking remained unchanged. There high and low, rich and poor, had only one idea of improving their political condition. The upper classes lived upon the prospect of regaining their former pre-eminence; and the lower, upon that of having the avenues to wealth and distinction reopened to them by the re-establishment of a native government. Even sensible and comparatively well-affected natives had no notion that there was any remedy for the existing depressed state of their nation except the sudden and absolute expulsion of the English. After that, I resided for some years in Bengal, and there I found quite another set of ideas prevalent among the educated natives. Instead of thinking of cutting the throats of the English, they were aspiring to sit with them on the grand jury or on the bench of magistrates. * * * *"

As said before, the majority of Anglo-Indian officers from interested motives were Anglicists and did not favour oriental education or cultivation of Indian vernaculars. Lord Bentinck was the chief of them.

The Charter Act of 1833 saddled India with the charge of the Indian Law Commission. Macaulay was the first member of this Commission. He came out to India to shake the pagoda tree and grow rich at the expense of the Indian natives. He was a very brilliant essayist, but from his writings he never made more than a couple of hundred pounds a year. So with no higher motive than that of accumulating 'filthy lucre,' he exiled himself to India. In a letter to his sister, who shared with him his self-imposed exile to India, he wrote :

"By the new India Bill, it is provided that one of the members of the Supreme Council, which is to govern our Eastern Empire, is to be chosen from among persons who are not servants of the Company. It is probably, indeed nearly certain, that the situation will be offered to me.

"The advantages are very great. It is a post of the highest dignity and consideration. The salary is ten thousand pounds a year. I am assured by persons who know Calcutta intimately, and who have themselves mixed in the highest circles and held the highest offices at the Presidency, that I may live in splendour there for five thousand a year, and may save the rest of the salary with the accruing interest. I may therefore hope to return to England at only thirty-nine, in the full vigour of life, with a fortune of thirty thousand pounds. * *

"I am not fond of money, or anxious about it. But, though every day makes me less and less eager for wealth, every day shows me more and more strongly how necessary a competence is to a man who desires to be either great or useful. * * I can live only by my pen: * * I have never made more than two hundred a year by my pen. I could not support myself in comfort on less than five hundred: and I shall in all probability have many others to support. The prospects of our family are, if possible, darker than ever."

The Education Committee was composed of both the parties of orientalists and occidentalists. The discussion regarding the oriental and occidental languages proceeded till the Committee became equally divided, and it was difficult to get even the ordinary business transacted. At this juncture Macaulay arrived in India in 1834. He knew nothing of Indian history and Indian literatures. He was not acquainted with any branch of Indian thought. Yet he was chosen by Lord Bentinck to decide the very important controversy between the occidentalists and orientalists. A worse selection could hardly have been made. Just as three decades back Bentinck as Governor of Madras selected Mr. Thackeray to write that report which declared that

"It is very proper that, in England, a good share

of the produce of the earth should be appropriated to support certain families in affluence, to produce senators, sages, and heroes for the service and defence of the State. * * * ;—but, in India, that haughty spirit of independence, and deep thought, which the possession of great wealth sometimes gives, ought to be suppressed. We do not want generals, statesmen, and legislators; we want industrious husbandmen."

Regarding the above, Mr. Digby in his Prosperous 'British India', wrote :

"Lord William Bentinck, * * of set purpose selected Mr. Thackeray as his mouthpiece, they holding ideas in common, * *"

Yes, in this instance also, Lord William Bentinck of set purpose selected Mr. Macaulay as his mouthpiece. The latter not only abused and insulted Indians—for no Indian or for the matter of that no Asiatic can read Macaulay's Minute without feeling deep humiliation,—but did all that lay in his power to suppress 'deep' thought among Indians by making them learn every thing through the medium of a foreign language like English.

Mr. Macaulay's Minute, though written in 1835, remained unpublished till 1864. His nephew, the present Sir George Otto Trevelyan, was the first to publish it in MacMillan's Magazine for May 1864.

"We are at present," Macaulay said, "a Board for Printing Books which are of less value than the paper on which they are printed was when it was blank, and for giving artificial encouragement to absurd history, absurd metaphysics, absurd physics, and absurd theology."

The Minute, if not actually written by Bentinck, must have been suggested by him. His lordship held his ideas in common with Macaulay. So Macaulay's Minute gladdened his lordship's heart to the utmost and one of the last acts of his administration was the promulgation of the following resolution on the part of the Supreme Government of British India :

Fort William, General Consultation.
7th March, 1835.

"The Governor-General of India in Council has attentively considered the two letters from the Secretary to the Committee, dated the 21st and 22nd January last, and the papers referred to in them.

"1st. His Lordship in Council is of opinion that the great object of the British Government ought to be the promotion of European literature and science among the natives of India; and that all the funds appropriated for the purposes of education would be best employed on English education alone.

"2nd. But it is not the intention of his Lordship in Council to abolish any college or school of native learning, while the native population shall appear to be inclined to avail themselves of the advantages which it affords; and his Lordship in Council directs that all the existing professors and students at all the institutions under the superintendence of the Committee shall continue to receive their stipends. But his Lordship in Council decidedly objects to the practice which has hitherto prevailed of supporting the students during the period of their education. He conceives that the only effects of such a system can be to give artificial encouragement to branches of learning which, in the natural course of things, would be superseded by more useful studies; and he directs that no stipend shall be given to any student that may hereafter enter at any of those institutions; and that when any professor of Oriental learning shall vacate his situation, the Committee shall report to the Government the number and state of the class, in order that the Government may be able to decide upon the expediency of appointing a successor.

"3rd. It has come to the knowledge of the Governor-General in Council that a large sum has been expended by the Committee on the printing of Oriental works; his Lordship in Council directs that no portion of the funds shall hereafter be so employed.

"4th. His Lordship in Council directs that all the funds which these reforms will leave at the disposal of the Committee be henceforth employed in imparting to the native population a knowledge of English literature and science, through the medium of the English language; and his Lordship in Council requests the

Committee to submit to Government, with all expedition, a plan for the accomplishment of this purpose."

" (Sd.) H. J. PRINSEP,
Secretary to Government."

Regarding Macaulay's Minute and Bentinck's resolution on the same, it is proper here to quote the opinion of Professor Horace Hayman Wilson. In his evidence before the Select Committee of the House of Lords on the Government of Indian Territories, Wilson on the 5th July, 1853 said :

" * * I have a great respect for Mr. Macaulay's talents but he was new in India, and he knew nothing of the people; he spoke only from what he saw immediately around him, which has been the great source of the mistakes committed by the advocates for English exclusively; they have known nothing of the country; they have not known what the people want; they only know the people of the large towns, where English is of use, and is effectively cultivated. But take the case of a young man, a student of the Hindoo College, become a Sudder Amin, who has gone into the Mofussil to administer justice—he does not meet with an individual who can converse with him in English, or knows anything about English. In all the transactions which come before him, he does not want English; what he wants is a thorough knowledge of his own language, of the law, and of the course of business, and the character of the people, formed as that is by Native, not English institutions; so that when you take the country at large, English is comparatively of no benefit, at least beyond the Presidencies and the large towns, where are our chief establishments and a European society.

"* * * * No doubt English ought to be encouraged as much as possible; but there was no necessity to limit our operations to that one object on the part of the advocates for the maintenance of the Native Colleges; there never was any disinclination to encourage and support in truth and earnestness the cultivation of English. All that they maintained was that we should not tie our hands up to either one or the other measure, but that we should avail ourselves of all available means for diffusing useful knowledge. Of course, that knowledge was to come from Europe. European literature and science were to form the basis and the bulk of the knowledge; but if we confined the knowledge to those alone who had the inclination and opportunity of acquiring English thoroughly, we confined it to a very limited class; in fact, we created a separate caste of English scholars, who had no longer any sympathy, or very little sympathy with their countrymen; whilst, if we could employ the services, as has been done by Mr. Ballantyne, at Benares, of the learned men of the country, we should have an additional instrument in our power, and one from which, perhaps, in the end the greater benefit of the two might arise."

But it was the policy of the authorities to create a separate caste, as it were, of English scholars who were expected not to have any or very little sympathy with their countrymen. Macaulay pleaded for English in the following terms :

"We must do our best to form a class who may be interpreters between us and the millions whom we govern; a class of persons Indian in blood and colour, but English in taste, in opinions, words, and intellect."

Regarding Macaulay's Minute, Wilson said :

"I have had an opportunity of reading it, and a very clever Minute it is; very ingenious, like all his writings; but there is throughout an evident want of experience and knowledge of the country."

Being asked,

"7208. Has not the order of Lord William Bentinck had any effect in increasing the study of the English language?"

H. H. Wilson said,

"In Bengal it may, but not in the Upper Provinces. The effects of that order have been very much misrepresented; the order itself was, in my opinion, an exceedingly objectionable one; it proposed to deprive the Native Colleges, the Sanskrit College of Calcutta, the Madressa and the Benares College, of the funds which had been appropriated to them by the liberality of the previous Governments, and to apply the whole to English education; it also deprived the students at those establishments of the provision which it had been the practice of Native Educational establishments to supply, the allowance of monthly stipends in lieu of maintenance—small scholarships, in fact, which were given to the students in consideration of their poverty; because, although belonging to the most respectable order of Native Society, they were generally the sons of poor people; they were not amongst the opulent people of India, any more than scholars in any other part of the world; and it was also considered advisable to hold out some encouragement of this kind to bring boys from a distance; so that those establishments should not be for the benefit solely of the inhabitants of Calcutta. * * * * These stipends, by Lord William Bentinck's order, were abolished entirely. The measure gave extreme dissatisfaction to the Native population; and very strong protests were made against it, particularly by the Mohammedans, who presented a petition, signed by above 8,000 of the most respectable people of Calcutta and the neighbourhood, protesting against the abolition of the stipends, and the withdrawal of the encouragement of Government from the Native establishments. In fact, the order was never carried into operation; for although it was not formally rescinded, yet in the subsequent administration of Lord Auckland it was essentially modified by the grant of pecuniary scholarships to a considerable number of the most industrious pupils in the Native establishments, as well as in the Hindoo College; these scholarships, therefore, in some degree compensated for the abolition of the stipends. Since that modification was introduced, the course of public instruction has gone on in the Native colleges without any complaint."

In reply to another question, Wilson said :

"Lord William Bentinck's order was to the effect, that it was his opinion that all the funds available for the purposes of education should be applied to the study of English alone; that was justly objected to by many of the members of the committee, who were best qualified to judge of its effect upon the minds of the people and upon the progress of education; for although the cultivation of English is, no doubt, very important, and ought to receive every possible assistance and countenance from the Government, yet it is not the means by which anything like a universal effect can be produced; it is not the means by which the people at large can be educated; in fact, no people can even become instructed or enlightened, except through their own language. It must be through the medium of their own language that you must address them, and disseminate useful knowledge amongst them. Their own forms of speech are, it is true, in a comparatively uncultivated state; but they may and will be improved by cultivation. * * * *"

Lord Elphinstone, one of the members of the Committee, asked Wilson,—

"7237. Was it not the fact that what Lord William Bentinck recommended was not the introduction of English to supersede the vernacular languages, but only the employment of English as a medium of education, instead of the Persian and the Sanskrit?"

"No, there was no qualification in regard to the vernacular languages; the order begins with this sentence, 'It is the opinion of the Governor-General that all funds which are available for the purposes of education should be applied to the cultivation of English alone." * * * *

The fact should not be lost sight of that the British administration of India had for its prototype that of Ireland. England tried to do in India what she had succeeded in doing in Ireland. So England's educational policy in heathen India was shaped, after that in Christian Ireland. Macaulay, who wrote the Education Minute of 1835, was inspired by the deeds of his countrymen in the field of education in Ireland. In his *English National Education* (p. 50) Prof. H. Holman writes :

"As far back as 1537 the Irish Parliament, acting under the English Privy Council, had founded parochial schools—*for the purpose of changing Irishmen into Englishmen, if that were possible.*"

Macaulay wrote in his Minute, as has already been quoted above, that the object was "to form a class of persons Indians in blood and colour, but English in taste, in opinions, words, and intellect."

In Macaulay's time, education in England belonged exculsively to the Church and the Church controlled the teaching. There was appointed the Board of Commissioners of National Education in Ireland. Prof. Holman writes :

"This board not only took over the entire management of the education of the poor, because the government was of opinion that no private society, deriving its income from 'private sources, and only made the channel of the munificence of the legislature without being subject to any direct responsibility, could adequately and satisfactorily accomplish the end proposed; ' but it dealt firmly with the question of religious instruction, laying down rules and regulations as to the time and manner for it, and actually compiling a book of 'Scripture extracts' to be read in schools, during the hours given to ordinary literary instruction. It issued a series of official school-books, and sold them to schools at reduced prices; and established a training college and normal schools; appointed inspectors to visit and report on the schools; and made grants for school buildings, and for increasing teachers' salaries." (*Ibid.*, p. 71).

Excepting 'scripture extracts' to be read in schools, almost everything that was done by the Board of Commissioners in Ireland was introduced in India by the Educational Minute of Lord Macaulay. It was only on the ostensible plea of religious toleration that 'scripture extracts' for reading in schools was not introduced.*

* This has since been done in recent years by the Calcutta University, which is an officially constituted body.

VERNACULAR EDUCATION IN THE DAYS OF THE EAST INDIA COMPANY.

At the present time many English statesmen and politicians declare themselves more in favour of education through the medium of the Indian vernaculars than through that of English. But no encouragement was held out to the cultivation of these vernaculars so long as the East India Company were the rulers of the country. Speaking of Shivaji, the late Revd. Dr. John Wilson of Bombay wrote :

"There can not be a doubt that the vernacular literature which had sprung up in the province to which he belonged, during the two centuries which preceded him, nursed the spirit of Hinduism in himself and his contemporaries, and was one of the main causes of their hatred of, and successful rebellion against the Muhammedan power which he was instrumental in heading."

A writer in the *Bombay Quarterly Review* for October, 1857 (page 322), quoting above, said :

"Will it [the vernacular literature] exercise any influence adverse to the British Government? Time will show."

It is evident that Dr. Duff and other Anglicists of those days were afraid of the growth of any vernacular literature in this country, for it might exercise some influence adverse to the British Government.

Macaulay was well versed in the history of his own country. It would seem that he came out to India to do what had been so successfully done in Ireland. It is a historical fact that,

"The English Government passed Acts of Parliament without number to suppress utterly the Irish language, ... In Elizabeth's time even the King of Denmark was refused by the English Government the services of an Irishman to translate Irish MSS., lest that should injure English interests! Henry the Eighth required a knowledge of English as the *sine qua non* for a Church-living in Ireland, he got men who knew nothing of the *people*. Subsequently it was enacted, in case the minister could not read the service in English, he might read it to the *people* in *Latin*, but not in Irish."*

A writer in the *Calcutta Review* for December, 1855, p. 309, said :

"History tells us, that no nation has ever yet been civilized or educated, save through its own vernacular, and that the uprooting of a vernacular is the extermination of the race, or at least of all its peculiar characteristics. Speech, Thought and Existence are so

* *Calcutta Review* for June, 1854, p. 306.

closely bound together, that it is impossible to separate them. They are the great trinity in unity of the race. If then we strive to up-root the vernacular of a country, or to deluge it not only with foreign modes of thought, but with foreign words, we shall either make no progress, or such a progress that we could speedily wish to undo it. But the Government system of Education has thus acted, * * * * and beginning at the wrong end—the top of the tree, they thought that like air-plants they would make education grow downward, and so had colleges without schools, and schools without primary schools, and Inspectors, with schools to create for their inspection. Making but one faint attempt to raise native teachers—an attempt that from the first contained in it the elements of its own destruction, they went on using foreigners and a foreign tongue, and a foreign literature, and thus never reached those inner springs of thought and action, that exist even in a Bengalee's soul, and will yet make a man of him and men of his nation."

To prevent adverse criticism, to conciliate those who had raised a hue and cry against the Anglicisation of Education, it was a grand stroke of policy which Bentinck adopted in deputing Mr. Adam to report on Vernacular Education in Bengal. Mr. Adam submitted three reports on the subject in 1835, 1836, 1838, and recommended

"Government to *afford encouragement to existing schools*, thus calling forth the efforts of the natives—

the preparation of improved class books—the appointment to each district of a native *examiner* of teachers and scholars, with an inspector to each five districts—*a model vernacular school in each district*, to which promising pupils from the ordinary schools should be admissible, to be paid small *stipends* in order to enable them to continue their studies."

A writer in the *Calcutta Review* for June, 1854 (No. XLIV), p. 324, commenting on the above, said :

"It is now 1854, sixteen years have elapsed, nothing has been done to carry out those plans in Bengal. Constituted as the Bengal Council of Education is, the members residing in Calcutta, a semi-Angilcized city, we could not expect them to take up with zeal vernacular education. Their first act in this case was to set aside Mr. Adam's plan, the only one feasible in this country. Mr. Macaulay, their president, knew nothing of the people; his knowledge of India was limited by the bounds of the Mahratta ditch. * * * * The Council have, however, in *words*, constantly held forth the necessity of 'the acquisition by the students, of a sufficient mastery of the Vernacular, to enable them to communicate with facility and correctness, in the language of the people, the knowledge obtained by them.'"

It was on the occasion of the renewal of the Charter in 1813 that the authorities of the East India Company had enjoined on the Governors of the different Presidencies in India to institute inquiries regarding the state of indigenous education in the different provinces of this country. This inquiry was neglected in Bengal. It was not until 1835, during the closing days of the administration of Lord William Bentinck, that Mr. Adam was appointed to undertake this enquiry. Mr. Adam had been at one time a Baptist Missionary, believing in the Trinity. But his meeting with the celebrated Ram Mohun Roy made him give up his belief in the Trinity and be converted to Unitarian Christianity. He was on this account nicknamed the "Second fallen Adam" by his charitable Christian countrymen. He edited with great ability *The India Gazette,* a popular Calcutta Journal.

Mr. Adam performed his task with great zeal and ability. The three reports which he drew up on the state of Education in Bengal and Behar contain a valuable mine of information on the contemporary state of instruction in native institutions and in native society. It is not necessary to refer to the contents of these reports at length. But it is necessary to mention what Mr. Adam found to be the vernacular media of instruction in Bengal Proper. According to him Bengali is

> "The language of the Musalman as well as of the Hindu population."

and that, though

"The Hindustani or Urdu is the current spoken language of the educated Musalmans of Bengal and Behar, it is never employed in the schools as the medium or instrument of written instruction. Bengali school books are employed by the Hindus of Bengal, and Hindi school books by the Hindus of Behar; but, although Urdu is more copious and expressive, more cultivated and refined than either, and possesses a richer and more comprehensive liiterature,* Urdu school books are wholly unknown. It is the language of conversation in the daily intercourse of life and in the business of the world, and it is the language also of oral instruction for the explanation of Persian and Arabic; but it is never taught or learned for its own sake or for what it contains."

A writer in the *Calcutta Review* for December, 1844 (Vol. II, p. 317), said :

"Educated Mussalmans, * * learn to speak and write the Bengali; and even several low castes of Hindus, occupying entire villages in various directions and amounting to several thousand individuals, whose ancestors three or four generations ago emigrated from the Western Provinces, have found it necessary to combine the use of Bengali with the Hindi, their mother-tongue. It thus appears that in the provinces of Bengal proper, the Bengali may justly be described as the universal language of vernacular instruction."

The argument of the Anglo-Indians, that

* This is no longer the case.

there being different languages used as vernaculars in a province, it was impossible to encourage them all, did not hold good so far as Bengal was concerned.

The Bengalee intellect was also of no mean order. In one of his reports, Mr. Adam wrote

"The native mind of the present day, although it is asleep, is not dead. It has a dreamy sort of existence in separating, combining, and recasting in various forms the fables and speculations of past ages. The amount of authorship shown to exist in the different distrists is a measure of the intellectual activity which, however now misdirected, might be employed for useful purposes. The same men who have wasted and are still wasting their learning and their powers in weaving complicated alliterations, recompounding absurd and vicious fictions, and revolving in perpetual circles of metaphysical abstractions, never ending still beginning, have professed to me their readiness to engage in any sort of literary composition that would obtain the patronage of Government."

The Indian vernaculars were neglected by the Indian authorities. Thus Mr. (afterwards Sir Frederick) Halliday, in his evidence before the Select Committee of the House of Commons on Indian Territories on the 25th July, 1853, on being asked by the Chaïrman,

"8788. I understand you to be in favour of the extension of tuition in the vernacular languages?"

answered,

"Very much so indeed; I am very desirous to see a great effort made in that direction; nothing serious has yet been done; the Government professes in all its schools and colleges to teach English and the Vernacular, but it does it imperfectly. Wherever Englisih is taught it swallows up everything else; the natives are so anxious to obtain it, and there is so much greater interest and excitement with respect to it on the part of those who are at the head of educational affairs, that there is more attention and more exertion bestowed upon education in English than upon education in the vernacular; and the whole of the means of education at their command being insufficient, the Vernacular is likely to be the more pinched of the two, so that that is not done which might be wished. In Lord Hardinge's time an attempt was made to establish a system of vernacular instruction; it was done in the face of great pecuniary difficulties; 101 schools were established, but the masters were very inadequately paid, and there were other errors in the management of the plan which, I think, caused it to fail. I will not conceal, that with some persons in India the failure of those schools has been thought to indicate that all such efforts towards vernacular education in Bengal must fail, but I am not one of those; on the contrary, I think the scheme failed on account of its inadequacy to the object in view, and that we are not the less bound, in consequence of the failure of that scheme, to do our best towards introducing, heartily and systematically, a good plan of vernacular education all over the country."

"8789. What gave rise to the plan of Lord Hardinge?—A general complaint that vernacular education was neglected, and a constant call upon the Government to do something towards extending Vernacular education; there happened to be at that moment certain funds temporarily at the disposal of the Governor of Bengal, which were applicable to that purpose, and he so applied them."

"8790. When you left Bengal, instruction in the vernacular languages was made secondary to instruction in English; was it not?—Quite so; more than secondary."

"8791. And that you think not desirable?—Not at all desirable; I think both are of enormous importance; there are parties in India who tell you the one thing needful is English instruction, and other parties who tell you the one thing needful is vernacular instruction. I differ with them both. I think the two ought to go on; they relate to different classes of the people altogether, and they ought to go on together. You ought, as far as possible, to give a good vernacular education to the masses, at the same time that you give opportunities to the classes who have leisure to do so, to acquire a knowledge of English literature and science."*

But it was considered incompatible with the 'enlightened selfishness'—we beg pardon—with the philanthropy of the Anglicists to encourage the cultivation of the Indian vernaculars. The

---

* Sixth Report from the Select Committee (House of Commons) on Indian Territories, 1853, pp. 59-60.

well-known Scotch Christian Missionary Dr. Duff was an earnest Anglicist. From such a man one should have expected fairness. But as a zealous Christian he perhaps thought it his duty to do everything that lay in his power to destroy 'heathen' institutions. And therefore he could not encourage the cultivation of Indian vernaculars. In a paper which was intended to be a defence of Lord Bentinck's resolution on Macaulay's Minute the reverend doctor wrote :

"The Act has been in substance styled, 'An Act of extermination against the Literature and Classical Languages of Hindustan.' * * * *

"Why, if common sense has not fled the habitations of man, this determination of withdrawing positive support is simply the restoration of the first position of strict neutrality; it is the resumption of an attitude of non-interference; it is a resolution to do nothing directly and actively, either to uphold or abolish native literature, so far as the British Government is concerned, it just leaves it precisely as it existed before its intervention at all; *i.e.*, it resigns the classical literature of India to the patronage and support of those who have cultivated and perpetuated the knowledge of it during the last thirty centuries.

* * * *

"If it could be shown that at any time when the British smote into the dust the confederacies of the Indian Rajahs and Nawabs, mounted the throne of the Great Mogul, and wielded the imperial sceptre over a domain more extensive, an empire more consolidated than that of the Mighty Aurangzeb, could it be proved that then, or at any subsequent period, the Government had really pledged itself, had actually entered into a solemn compact with the representatives of the people of India, to devote *in perpetuity* a determinate amount of funds for the specific purpose of encouraging native literature in certain native institutions; then, indeed, but not till then, would the sudden or gradual withdrawment of such funds implicate the good faith, the honour or the justice of the British Government."*

The Calcutta Review for June, 1854, No. XLIV, p. 297, wrote:

"It has been said, do nothing to enlighten the masses, till you give a high education to a number, and these will educate the masses—we do not object to the former, but we do not postpone the latter to an indefinite period. To enlighten only the few is, to use a Hindu proverb, to sweeten the ocean by casting a few drops of milk on it. The rush for keraniships with their deadening effects, and the want of *practical* education among Hindus, show that vernacular education should have been combined with the English. The Government began in 1835 with educating the few,—is not the time now arrived, in 1854, after a lapse of twenty years, for not ending there, but extending education to the *many?* To wait until our English students awake from the torpor of keraniship, until they

---

* The Lords' Committee's Second Report on Indian Territories, 1853, pp. 406-7.

renounce the selfishness of making a monopoly of knowledge, will, we fear, be like Horace's rustic—waiting to cross the river until it dries up. To carry out the principle of enlightening *only* the few at first, we ought to have Colleges before schools, and even an university before a college. We see the case of France, where there was *a highly refined nobility*, that of the days of Louis le Grand, the *salons* of Paris were the resort of a brilliant class of *savans*, but the peasantry were kept in a state of awful ignorance—revolution broke out, and all this drapery of refinement was torn to shreds before the whirlwind of infuriated masses, discharging a lava of passions uncontrolled by any barriers of knowledge. The aristocracy (the Young Bengal of that day), who kept the peasantry debarred from knowledge, were startled from their dream of fancied security by the flames of their castles and midnight yell of '*la paix aux Chaumieres, la guerre aux Chateaux*'—a warning voice, that the mere education of the few is a vineyard clothing the volcanoe's side, * * * * of late years, notwithstanding the influence of our universities and classical schools, what awful disclosures have the Earl of Shaftesbury and the promoters of ragged schools made, as to the condition of the working classes, and the dense ignorance and crime which even still form the substratum of English society; an able writer in the *Agra Messenger* remarks on this subject, 'when we know how little the English universities, colleges, and great public scools *existing through centuries*, have done for the *people* of England, we cannot hope that a similar system in India, where the barriers of caste strengthen the wall of partition betwixt the *educated few* and the ignorant many, will produce more satisfactory results. The light of knowledge naturally burns upward. It was only when the *National Schools, Sunday Schools, Mechanics' Institutes*, began to spread their influence among the labouring body in England, that the people received anything like enlightenment. But even these agencies left a yet lower class in darkness, to be in time illuminated by the heroic teachers of ragged Schools.' Knowledge made a monopoly of by a few, and invested with power, is an instrument of despotism, as the Histories of Chaldea, India, Persia, Egypt, and the Middle Ages show, and we say with Mr. Hodgson in his letters, that 'making knowledge an official monopoly, in the hands of a small number of people, is not identifying the security of our dominion with the happiness of the mass of the subjects.' Do not the waters of knowledge, restrained in a limited space, stagnate, whereas when diffused like the ocean, they become the purifiers of the world? In 1848 the Government of the N. W. Provinces very properly expressed their fears 'that the village and district officers will be so far ahead of the mass of the people, as the more to expose the latter to injury from dishonesty and intrigues.' * * In Ireland on the other hand, we have had for centuries intelligent but tyrannical landlords, who ruled, with a rod of iron, the tenantry they abandoned to ignorance.

"* * Young Bengal, equally with proud Brahman, despises 'the *vulgar* tongue, reminding us of the English squires in Locke's days, who could not write correct English,—though they could 'sport Latin verses.' And this is justified on the plea that there is so little in Bengali to read. Well, supposing it to be so— is not this, on the principle that 'it is more blessed to give than to receive a reason why the language should be enriched by those who have got the wealth of another tongue? Did Dante and Chaucer despise their own tongues because they were poor?—No! that was just the stimulus to prompt them to raise them.

"Of course, those natives who wish their sons to get employment in offices, where a knowledge of English is requisite, would wish all the Government funds for education, to be given to English schools, the high road to affluence,'—forgetting that the land revenue of Bengal amounts to three and a half millions sterling, besides five millions from salt and opium, and that the peasantry have a claim on those revenues for an education suited to their circumstances, a *quid pro quo.* * * And yet, for sooth, all knowledge is to be excluded, unless the people will sit down to an eight years' study of foreign language, with its arbitrary pronunciation and intricacy of meaning. English Education, to affect the mass, must have a vernacular medium—oil by itself will not mix with water.

"If we are to do nothing in Vernacular Education until the upper classes are enlightened by English, then let us be consistent, let us stop our Bible Societies, Vernacular Literature Committees, Tract Societies, for they will be of very little use, if there be not a correspondent system of Vernacular Education. Can we reckon that those few will carry out the principle of 'doing what they can for the benefit of their less favoured neighbours?' Does not the voice of history show that there are aristocrats in knowledge, who fear lest 'the peasants' toe should tread on the courtier's heel.'"

One of Macaulay's motives in introducing English Education in India was that such a step would help in the conversion of Indians to Christianity, a hope never adequately fulfilled. Thus in 1836 he wrote to his father that

"The effect of this education on the Hindus is prodigious. No Hindu who has received an English education ever remains sincerely attached to his religion. Some continue to profess it as a matter of policy, but many profess themselves pure Deists and some embrace Christianity. *It is my firm belief if our plans of education are followed up there will not be a single idolater among the respectable classes in Bengal thirty years hence.**

Here also Macaulay tried to copy the Educational Policy then in vogue in his country. The author of *English National Education* (p. 72) writes:

"The general character of the claims of the High

---

* *The Indian Daily News* for March 30, 1909, from which the above extract is made, truly observes:—"Lord Macaulay's triumph over the Oriental School, * * was really the triumph of a deliberate intention to undermine the religious and social life of India. It is no doubt a hard thing to say that this was not merely the consequence of his act but that it was also his deliberate intention, but the * * letter written in 1836 to his father shows how behind his splendid phrases, there lay quite a different view."

Church party is shown by the words of its leader. Keble boldly declared that England 'as a Christian nation was a part of Christ's Church, and bound in all her legislation, by the fundamental laws of that Church.' . . . . That the State should profess, and cause to be taught, at least the Christian faith was, practically, held by all intelligent and worthy men."

Again on p. 73 of the above mentioned work, Prof. Holman writes :

"In the preface to a published sermon, preached in February, 1838, Bishop Blomfield writes :—'No system of education can be forced upon the people at large which shall not be in conformity with the principles of the Church of England, and worked by its instrumentality. It will be our own fault if it be otherwise.' In the sermon itself he frankly declares: 'We assert that *this* [the imparting of the rudiments of knowledge] is not to be the main and primary much less the sole, object of our endeavours, in educating the youth of this country, of whatever class they may be'."

But the Anglicists probably meant to prevent the growth of Indian nationality and therefore they made use of arguments and language to serve their ulterior ends. This is evident from what Dr. Duff further wrote in the paper already referred to above. He wrote :

"The vast influence of language in moulding national feeling and habits, more especially if fraught with superior stores of knowledge, is too little attended to, and too inadequately understood. * * When the Romans conquered a province, they forthwith set themselves to the task of 'Romanising' it; that is, they strove to create a taste for their own more refined language and literature, and thereby aimed at turning the song and the romance and the history—the thought and the feeling and fancy of the subjugated people into Roman channels, which fed and augmented Roman interests. And has Rome not succeeded? Has she not saturated every vernacular dialect with which she came in contact with terms copiously drawn from her own? Has she not perpetuated for ages, after her sceptre moulders in the dust, the magic influence of her character and name? Has she not stamped the impress of her own genius on the literature and the laws of almost every European Kingdom with a fixedness that has remained unchanged up to the present hour?

"And who can tell to what extent the strength and perpetuity of the Arabic domination is indebted to the Caliph Walid, who issued the celebrated decree, that the language of the Koran should be the universal language of the Mahomedan world, so that from the Indian Archipelago to Portugal it actually became the language of religion, of literature, of Government, and generally of common life?"

"And who can estimate the extent of influence exerted in India by the famous Edict of Akbar, the greatest and the wisest far of the sovereigns of the House of Timur? Of this Edict, an authority * * wrote, * * 'The great Akbar established the Persian language as the language of business and of polite literature throughout his extensive dominions, and the popular tongue naturally became deeply impregnated with it. The literature and the language of the country thus became identified with the genius of his dynasty; *and this has tended more than anything else to produce a kind of intuitive veneration for the family, which has long survived even the destruction of their power; and this feeling will continue to exist until we substitute the English language for the Persian,* which will dissolve the spell, and direct the ideas and sympathies of the natives towards their present rulers.'

"* * He (Lord Bentinck) it was who first resolved to supersede the Persian, in the political department of the public service, by the substitution of the English, * * ; and having thus by one act created a necessity and consequently, an increased and yearly increasing demand for English, he next consummated the great design by superadding the enactment under review which provides the requisite means for supplying the demand that had been previously created; and this united Act now bids fair to outrival in importance the Edicts of the Roman, the Arabic and the Mogul Emperors, inasmuch as the English language is infinitely more fraught with the seeds of truth in every province of literature, science and religion, than the languages of Italy, Arabia or Persia ever were. Hence it is that I venture to hazard the opinion, that Lord W. Bentinck's double Act for the encouragement and diffusion of the English language and English literature in the East; will, long after contemporaneous party interests, and individual jealousies, and ephemeral rivalries have sunk into oblivion, be hailed by a grateful and benefited posterity as the grandest masterstroke of sound policy that has yet characterized the administration of the British Government in India."*

From the above it is quite evident that the Anglicists strove from interested motives to make English the medium of instruction in Indian schools and colleges. They were not actuated by any altruistic or philanthropic considerations to diffuse English education in India but to "direct the ideas and the sympathies of the natives towards their present rulers."

But it was impossible for the English to do what the Caesars, the Caliphs and Akbar and Jehangir did. The people of England lack sympathetic imagination and therefore it is impossible for them to anglicise their Indian fellow-subjects.† As a native of Scotland, Dr. Alexander Duff lacked imagination and therefore he failed to imagine the non-possibility of his co-religionists and compatriots being able to do what the Romans, Arabs and Moguls did.

Regarding the British Government of India, the late Mr. R. C. Dutt in one of his speeches said:

---

* *Ibid*, p. 409.

† "The Anglo-Saxon nations," writes Lecky, "though sometimes roused to strong but transient enthusiasm, are habitually singularly narrow, unappreciative, and unsympathetic."

EXCLUSIVE RULE UNEXAMPLED IN HISTORY.

Gentlemen, history records scarcely any example of a great and civilised nation permanently placed under a system of government which allowed them no share in the control over their own concerns. In ancient India, the entire village administration was in the hands of village communities or local landlords, and though there was no representation in its modern forms kings and potentates listened to the wishes of the people and the leaders of the people in deciding on great questions of administration. In ancient Europe the policy of Imperial Rome was inspired by the same spirit, and you no doubt recollect the eloquent words in which Gibbon has described the treatment of conquered provinces by Rome:—

"The grandsons of the Gauls, who had besieged Julius Caesar in Alesia, commanded legions, governed provinces, and were admitted into the Senate of Rome. Their ambition, instead of disturbing the tranquillity of the State, was intimately connected with its safety and greatness."

The history of Moghul Rule in India may also be described in almost the same words, and we can truly say:—

"The grandsons of the Hindus who had fought against Babar in the field of Fatehpur Sikri, commanded legions, governed provinces, and were admitted into the Councils of Akbar. Their ambition, instead of disturbing the tranquillity of the State, was intimately connected with its safety and greatness."

Shall we for ever continue to describe British Rule in India in words the reverse of this? Shall we for ever have to say:—

"The grandsons and great-grandsons of those who helped the British in the fields of Plassey and Wandewash, of Laswari and Assye, were excluded from the command of armies, from the government of provinces, from the Council of the Secretary of State for India, from the Executive Council of the Viceroy, from the Executive Councils of the Indian provinces."*

Gentlemen, this defect in British rule, this reproach of British administration, cannot last. One of the strongest of British Imperialists of modern days has recorded:—

"To those who take a purely selfish view, it may be urged that we can hardly long go on as we are, refusing to proceed further in the direction of the employment of natives in high office, with Russians at our door pursuing the other policy. * * * The unshared rule of a close bureaucracy from across the seas cannot last in the face of widespread modern education of a people so intelligent as Indian Natives."

The inhabitants of England, in whatever capacity they come to India, whether as public servants of the State or merchants or missionaries, do not make India their homes. So they cannot be the objects of that veneration which the descendants of Akbar even after the destruction of their power received from the Hindoos.

* Indians are not now entirely excluded from these councils.

The Caliphs civilized the Christian nations of Syria, Egypt, Northern Africa and even of Spain and Portugal. The Arabs or Saracens, as they were latterly called, behaved in such a chivalrous manner that the Christian women of those countries willingly became the inmates of their harems and gladly accepted the crescent in the place of the cross. Even in the last century, Lady Ellenborough deserted her legally married Christian husband and preferred to become the inmate of the seraglio of a Muhammadan Arab. It was not all by the confiscation of the women of the Christian countries that Islam succeeded in exterminating Christianity in the countries bordering the Mediterranean. Of course, the author of the Conflict between Religion and Science writes :

> "A nation may recover the confiscation of its provinces, the confiscation of its wealth; it may survive the imposition of enormous war-fines; but it never can recover from that most frightful of all war-acts, the confiscation of its women. * * It was the institution of polygamy, based upon the confiscation of the women in the vanquished countries, that secured for ever the Mohammedan rule. The children of these unions gloried in their descent from their conquering fathers. No better proof can be given of the efficacy of this policy than that which is furnished by North Africa. The irrestible effect of polygamy in consoli-

dating the new order of things was very striking. In little more than a generation, the Khalif was informed by his officers that the tribute must cease, all the children born in that region were Mohammedans, and all spoke Arabic."*

But it is impossible to imagine that those countries would have become Muhammadanized by mere confiscation of their women folk if those Christian women were not willing to tender their persons to their Muhammadan conquerors. India never became a Muhammadan country by the 'confiscation' of her women. No. Hindoo women cheerfully mounted the funeral pyre and reduced themselves to ashes rather than suffer themselves to be polluted by the touch of any conqueror.

The thorough Anglicisation of the whole of India is not desired by Anglo-Indians. In his *New India*, Cotton has written :

"The more Anglicised a native is, the more he is disliked by Englishmen. The sense of jealousy becomes greater. Whatever may be professed, Englishmen are ready to encourage the natives who speak broken English more than those who speak good English; those who are subject to Hindu prejudices more than those who have renounced them; and generally those who are far removed from English habits of thought and life more than those who have made a

---

* Draper, pp. 100-1.

very close approach to them. They are more pleased with the backward Hindu than with his advanced compatriot, because the former has made no attempt to attain equality with themselves.

"This abhorrence of equality rankles in the mind of. all Anglo-Indians, and especially of officials. It is the peculiarity of residence in the East to develop sentiments of intolerance and race superiority."*

Such being the feelings of the Anglo-Indians towards Indians, it is impossible for English people to succeed like the Romans, the Caliphs or the Moghuls in "anglicising" the whole of India.

But there can be no doubt that the occidentalists or the Anglicists made English the medium of instruction for Indian scholars to prevent the cultivation of Indian vernaculars, and thus of Indian nationality, but also "aimed at turning * * * the thought and the feeling and fancy of the subjugated people into" English channels, to feed and augment English interests, and to "direct the ideas and sympathies of the natives towards their present rulers."

Whatever promotes better understanding between different races is bound to produce good results. Therefore, whatever the motives of the Anglicists in the days of the East India

* New India (Second Edition), 1886, pp. 40-1.

Company might have been, our knowledge of the English language and literature has borne good fruit. The Anglicists have builded better than they knew or perhaps meant to. English education has been one of the causes of the birth of national consciousness in India. If now the vernaculars be encouraged instead of English, the ultimate result will be a further impetus to the growth of national feeling. Directly or indirectly, whatever the educational policy adopted, it is destined to play a leading part in the progressive nationalisation of the Indian people.

EDUCATION OF INDIANS 1833—1853.

The Anglicists were triumphant, for Bentinck issued the resolution "that all the funds appropriated for the purposes of education would be best employed on English education alone." The authorities were averse to diffuse education among the masses of the Indian population. Lord Bentinck himself was not in favour of widely educating Indians. His successor Metcalfe had expressed himself strongly in favour of education. While recommending an improved system of revenue settlement, he wrote as follows :

"Similar objections have been urged against our attempting to promote the education of our native subjects, but how unworthy it would be of a liberal Government to give weight to such objections! The world is governed by an irresistible power which giveth and taketh away dominion, and vain would be the impotent prudence of man against the operations of its almighty influence. All that rulers can do is to merit dominion by promoting the happiness of those under them. If we perform our duty in this respect, the gratitude of India, and the admiration of the world, will accompany our name through all ages, whatever may be the revolutions of futurity; but if we withhold blessings from our subjects, from a selfish apprehension of possible danger at a remote period, we shall not deserve to keep our dominion, we shall merit that reverse which time has possibly in store for us, and shall fall with the mingled hatred and contempt, hisses and execrations of mankind."*

But as Governor-General of India, he did very little to promote education. Of course, it was from considerations of "enlightened selfishness," that it was thought necessary to give some sort of eduoation to Indians. Such education was to be given as would produce cheap clerks and useful subordinates for service in the different departments of the State. With that object in view, Lord Hardinge wrote a Minute, dated 10th October, 1844, extracts from which are given below :

"The Governor--General, having taken into consideration the existing state of education of Bengal, and being of opinion that it is highly desirable to afford it every reasonable encouragement by holding out to those who have taken advantage of the opportunity of instruction a fair prospect of employment in the public service, and thereby not only to reward individual merit but to enable the State to profit as largely as possible by the result of the measures adopted of late years for the instruction of the people as well by the Government as by private individuals and societies, has resolved that in every possible case a preference shall be given in the selection of candidates

---

* Pp. 46-7 of Kaye's Selections from the Writings of Metcalfe.

for public employment to those who have been educated in the institutions thus established, and especially to those who have distinguished themselves therein by a more than ordinary degree of merit."

The sum appropriated to education was very inadequate. Mr. J. C. Marshman, in his evidence on 21st July, 1853, before the Select Committee of the House of Commons on Indian Territories, said :

" It was stated in the House of Commons that the sum appropriated to education by the Government of India did not exceed £65,000 sterling a year; but in a series of papers published at the India House in the present year, the sum was stated at between £70,00 and £80,000. Dr. Wilson, in his evidence, I see, has brought in the sum of 10,000 rupees appropriated to Scinde, and 70,000 rupees to Sattara, which were evidently not included in that calculation. The sum, therefore, may be taken at £89,000 or £90,000 sterling per annum. If you compare the sum thus devoted from the revenues of India to the object of public instruction, with that which is voted by Parliament annually from the revenues of England for education in this country, I think it will be found to be very considerably disproportionate. If you assume the revenues of England at £52,000,000 sterling, and the sum appropriated annually by Parliament at £250,000 sterling, which, I think, is very nearly the sum, then from the £26,000,000 net revenue in India we ought to obtain £125,000, and therefore if we have only £90,000 we are still, according to that proportion, some £35,000 or 40,000 below the mark. But even that sum is insufficient for the wants of the country, and I am satisfied that if it were quadrupled, or increased even five-fold, it would not be found too much for the educational necessities of the country; and it is especially to be desired that there should also be an attempt at the same time, to make those additional funds go as far as possible by a new mode of appropriating them."

Then he was asked—

"8615. What mode of dispensing educational funds in India do you contemplate?"

In reply he said—

"* * * if we could also borrow the plan adopted by the Privy Council of Education in this country, of giving Grants-in-aid to the various institutions in India, those funds might be made to go much further, and that this would be a more appropriate mode of expending any additional funds which might be voted, than by exclusively following the present mode. It is scarcely possible for the Government in India to undertake the care and the responsibility of managing all the institutions which will be necessary for the diffusion of knowledge, and there is a general desire in India, in the minds of almost all parties, that the Government could be prevailed on to adopt the principle of Grants-in-aid; that is, they should determine to give pecuniary assistance to the existing institutions which are not connected with the State, in order to enable them to increase the sphere of their exertions. In that case it would be necessary for the Govenment to prescribe the course of study, and possibly even to lay down the books which should be used, and that an inspector should be employed to visit every school thus taken under the patronage of this Government, three or four times a year, and make a report of the progress of the children; the Government aid to the institution being proportioned according to the report made by the inspector. This would produce the double effect of giving an extraordinary impulse to the cause of education in India, at the same time that it would give the means of support to those institutions which can scarcely obtain adequate encouragement from local subscriptions."

The witness was a son of the well-known Serampore Missionary—one of the trio—Revd. Mr. Marshman. When he made that recommendation of Grants-in-aid, he had an ulterior end to serve. What this was may be gathered from the answer to a further question when he said that—

"The Government would thus be enabled to give assistance even to Christian schools and institutions, without in any measure infringing that principle of religious neutrality which has been always adopted, and which is a very great element of our political strength."

Although the Government did not do anything for the diffusion of education, private enterprise was not idle, at least in Bengal, for the cause of education. The most notable institution established during this period was the Hooghly College. It was founded with funds furnished by the munificence of a Muhammadan gentleman named Haji Muhammad Mohsin. This seminary of learning has done much for the education of Muhammadans and one of the most notable Muhammadans of Bengal—a man of very humble origin—owed his education to this institution. The Right Honorable Mr. Syed Amir Ali was one of the alumni of the Hooghly College.

During the twenty years under review the Indian Government as in the previous twenty years did very little for the diffusion of general education among the people of this country. That was left to the people themselves. And to their credit let it be said that they performed their part very creditably The vernaculars were shame- very creditably. The vernaculars were shamefully neglected. A Christian Missionary like Dr. Duff even went the length of advising the Government to preserve strict neutrality regarding the vernaculars, that is to say, not to give any helping hand for their cultivation. True it is that the general Committee of Public Instruction of The Presidency of Fort William in Bengal, in their Report for the year 1835, wrote :

"We are deeply sensible of the importance of encouraging the cultivation of the vernacular languages. We do not conceive that the order of the 7th of March precludes us from doing this, and we have constantly acted on this construction. In the discussions which preceded that order, the claims of the vernacular languages were broadly and prominently admitted by all parties, and the question submitted for the decision of Government only concerned the relative advantage of teaching English on the one side, and the learned Eastern languages on the other. We therefore conceive that the phrases 'European literature and science,' 'English education alone,' and 'imparting to the native population a knowledge of English literature and science, through the medium of the English language,' are intended merely to secure the preference to European learning, taught through the medium of the English language, over Oriental learning, taught through the medium of the Sanskrit and Arabic languages, as regards the instruction of those natives who receive a learned education at our seminaries. These expressions have, as we understand them, no reference to the question through what ulterior medium such instruction as the mass of the people is capable of receiving is to be conveyed. If English had been rejected, and the learned Eastern tongues adopted, the people must equally have received their knowledge, through the vernacular dialects. It was, therefore, quite unnecessary for the Government, in deciding the question between the rival languages, to take any notice of the vernacular tongues; and, consequently, we have thought that nothing could reasonably be inferred from its omission to take such notice.

"We conceive the formation of a vernacular literature to be the ultimate object to which all our efforts must be directed. At present, the extensive cultivation of some foreign language, which is always very improving to the mind, is rendered indispensable by the almost total absence of a vernacular literature, and the consequent impossibility of obtaining a tolerable education from that source only. The study of English, to which many circumstances induce the natives to give the preference, and with it the knowledge of the learning of the West, is therefore daily spreading. This, as it appears to us, is the first stage in the process by which India is to be enlightened. The natives must learn before they can teach. The best educated among them must be placed in possession of our knowledge before they can transfer it into their own language. We trust that the number of such translations will now multiply every year. As the superiority of European learning becomes more generally appreciated, the demand for them will no doubt increase, and we shall be able to encourage any good books which may be brought out in the native languages by adopting them extensively in our seminaries."

It is stated in the *Calcutta Review* for June, 1854, No. XLIV, p. 305 :

"In Bengal, with its thirty-seven millions, the Government bestows 8,000 rupees annually on Vernacular Education! One-third the salary of a Collector of the revenue! As much is expended on 200 prisoners in jails. How different is it in America. Siljestom in his *Educational Institutions of the United States*, remarks:—

"'In America, popular education has from the beginning been based upon the idea of citizenship, not of philanthropy. There the gift of education to the people has not been considered merely as an act of charity to the poor, but as a privilege which every citizen as such, had a right to claim, and a duty which, by virtue of the social contract, every citizen binds himself to fulfil; and for the purpose of bestowing such education, (that is to say, the minimum of knowledge which every citizen ought to possess), the State is entitled to tax the community; whereas, the higher branches of education, which only a small number of the people have the means of acquiring, have been looked upon as matters concerning only those individuals who are anxious to avail themselves thereof, and have in consequence been left to private enterprise; the general force of circumstances, and the encouragement held out by the emoluments bestowed by the State on its servants, being regarded as sufficient inducements to those who aspire to enter the public service, to acquire the necessary knowledge. The immediate consequences hereof are, that while in America we find most excellent popular schools, maintained at the expense of the State, there are but few institutions connected with the higher branches of education which do not owe their origin and maintenance solely to the exertions of individuals or private associations.'"

But, as shown by the evidence of Mr. Halliday, no encouragement was given by the authorities in India to the vernaculars. Their cultivation was left to the natives. And how creditably they performed their task is evident from the evidence of Mr. J. C. Marshman before the Select Committee of the House of Commons on Indian Territories on 21st July, 1853. He said :

"The difficulty which was felt 10 or 12 years ago regarding books for a course of vernacular education is rapidly disappearing; and at the present time, if the Government were prepared to give suitable encouragement, that is to say, to the extent of £1,000 or £1,500 sterling, for the translation of the books which might be required, in the course of three or four years it would have as complete a vernacular school library as could be desired at present.

* * * *

"Those who have been opposed to vernacular education, and are for confining all their exertions to English instruction, have been in the habit of decrying translations; but there can be no reason why a translation of a good work on history, or geography, or astronomy should not be quite as useful as the original. Our own literature, although it contains the finest classics, is at the present time enriched by translations from the German, and that literature itself began three or four centuries ago in translations. If the Committee will allow me, I will read a short extract from

Wharton, who in his 'History of English Poetry,' says, 'Caxton, by translating, and procuring to be translated a great number of books from the French, greatly contributed to promote the state of literature in England.' This was the mode in which our literature, now so rich and complete, commenced, and it is the mode in which vernacular literature, more especially for schools, must commence in India. I think it is worthy of remark, that as the natives do necessarily receive their knowledge of our laws, in which all their interests are bound up, through the means of translations, there can be no reason whatever why they should not be able to receive the main facts of history, geography, and astronomy through the same medium."

But the Indian authorities did nothing to encourage the cultivation of the vernaculars. Perhaps it was not considered politically expedient to do so. Or it may be that some of the Anglicists wanted to suppress the vernaculars and thought it possible that these languages could be extinguished. For the Chairman asked Mr. Marshman—

"8632. There has been an idea that the spread of English will gradually supersede the use of the vernacular dialects in India, and obviate the necessity of cultivating them; do you share that opinion?"

Mr. Marshman in reply said,—

"Not at all; I do not think it is borne out by experience; certainly not by the experience which we have in Bengal. It is impossible to extinguish the language of 30,000,000 people; English will, doubtless in the course of time, become the classical language of Bengal, and every native of respectability will endeavour to give a knowledge of it to his children; but at the same time, the vernacular language of Bengal, and that of the North-Western Provinces, and of the other provinces throughout India, will continue to be used and to be cultivated to an increasing degree. In fact, as the Government have abolished the Persian language, and made the vernacular language of each province the language of the Courts and of public business, those languages become permanently and for ever fixed in the habits of the people. *I do not think there is an adequate idea in this country of the extent to which the Bengalee language is at the present time cultivated and employed by the natives themselves. We have found that in exact proportion to the efforts which are made for the dissemination of the English language, the adherence of the natives to their old language, and their anxiety to improve and to use it, to continually increasing.* In the year 1800, when the Serampore missionaries first began their labours, and set about the civilisation (?) and evangelisation of the province of Bengal, they found that there was not a single printed book in Bengalee extant, with the exception of the laws of the Government, and one dictionary. There was not a prose work existing in the Bengalee language, and they had everything to create. They employed the ablest native to compose works, and it was from their press that the first publications were issued. About 13 years ago, the Committee of Public Instruction published a list of the works in the Bengalee language which they found then existing; that is, 40 years after the Serampore missionaries had begun to print books in the language; and they found that there were 50 works which had been issued under the auspices of Europeans, and 173 which had been published by the natives themselves. If the Committee will permit me, I will quote a remark which was made by an influential paper, on the first announcement of this fact: 'Many of these works are, it is true, composed of the most contemptible trash; others, and by far too large a portion of them, consist of amatory poems; but many are of a higher character, and contain disquisitions on law, religion, metaphysics, medicine, and philosophy. With this list before us, we ask whether a language which has already received such a degree of cultivation as to be capable of conveying ideas to the mind on so large a variety of subjects, of which some are not wanting in abstruseness, can be that poor, meagre, wretched, inefficient tongue which some of the patrons of English have taken it to be; whether a language which can express the subtlties of law and philosophy, and can impart the enthusiasm of poetry, and give a stimulus to the most voluptuous imagination, does stand in need of a whole century of improvement before it can be fit for the purposes of national education.' This report was published by the Committee about 12 years ago. Last year a friend of mine made a collection of all the books that could be obtained in the Bengalee language, and he found that the number of works had been multiplied to 400; and at the present time there are no less than 40 native presses in Calcutta, continually employed by the natives themselves in the publication of books. The number of volumes sold the year before last amounted to no less than 30,000; and hence, notwithstanding the endeavour to diffuse English throughout the country, the Bengalee language is a more powerful medium of impression on the native mind even than Engliish. I think that with the advantages which the Government have just given to the natives of the country, by introducing a liberal system for the transmission of books at a low price, the native press is likely to receive an astonishing impulse."

Had the vernaculars been employed as the media of instruction, their cultivation would have progressed by leaps and bounds, and very useful literature on every subject would have been produced in them. It is the demand which creates the supply. There being no demand for useful works in our vernaculars, it is small wonder that is had hardly any decent vernacular literature to boast of. In 1853 the Japanese language was not half so well advanced as Bengalee, Hindee or other leading vernacular dialects of India. If useful literature in Japanese has since been cultivated, there is no reason why the same should not have taken place in our vernaculars also had they been properly encouraged. But the cultivation of the vernaculars was left to the people themselves.

Thus it would be seen that neither in the dissemination of general education nor in the cultivation of our vernaculars, the people of India during 20 years, *i.e.*, from 1833—1853 received that amount of patronage and aid from the Government of their country which every civilised government is bound to render to its subjects.

There was established a Bengal Vernacular Society, regarding whose programme, the *Calcutta Review* for 1851 wrote as follows :

PROGRAMME OF THE BENGAL VERNACULAR SOCIETY, 1851.

"It has been objected by some, that translations into the vernaculars are absurd, because they cannot transfuse all the shades of thought of the original; that the Bengali is the rude tongue of a semi-barbarous race; that dialects are already too numerous in India; and that we ought to abandon translations, and teach the people through English alone.

* * * *

"We shall take up the various objections urged against the vernacular Translation Society *seriatim*.

"1. 'There are so many dialects in India.'—There are only *five* principal tongues to a population of 150 millions;—Bengali, the language of 25 millions, Urdu, spoken from Cape Comorin to the Himalayas, Telugu, Tamil, and Mahratta. Now the Delhi Vernacular Translation Society's labours may be of use to 30 millions and those of the Bengal Translation

Society to 25 millions—a greater number than speak the Dutch, Italian, Spanish, Portuguese, Danish, Swedish, and Polish languages respectively. Would any of the nations using these languages tolerate a proposition, that no translations should be made into them, because they are used by a limited number? Are we to have no translations made from German or French into English, because the number of readers is limited? So far from it—we see even our American friends devoting a considerable expenditure of time and money to a series of translations from German into English, even though only a limited number will avail themselves of these.

"2. 'The Bengali is the rude dialect of a semi-barbarous race.'—We leave the Bengalis themselves, on the ground of patriotism or nationality, to deal with the latter part of this proposition. But, we ask, can that be a rude dialect, which has been made to convey, expressively and suitably, the truths of natural history, chemistry, natural philosophy, mental philosophy, and above all, which has been found fully equal to express the mysterious dogmas of revelation, the lyric effusions of Isaiah, and the lofty strains of the minor prophets of a Scripture? Besides, the Bengali, in its derivation from that noble tongue, the Sanskrit, possesses unbounded resources for borrowing terms and phraseology and is gradually increasing in its capabilities. The Moslem power has not been able to extirpate it, and all the energy of an Aurungzebe could not drive it from the homes and hearts of the people. By its close affinity with their venerated Sanskrit, it preserves the lingering rays of the long-faded glories of their ancient literature. Without touching on its merits as a translation, we would refer to Yates's translation of the Bible in Bengali as a monument of the degree of elegance and expressiveness to which the Bengali language has attained.

"3. 'We ought to teach all the natives through English; and then translation would not be necessary.'—We do not now treat of what is *desirable*, but of what is *practicable*. We think it very desirable that there were only one language in the world, and regret that the confusion of tongues ever took place; but we have to deal with a different state of things. We are in a country, where the Europeans are but a handful compared with the natives; where we have to encounter the antipathies arising from difference of race, creed, manners; and where, with few exceptions, the Hindus regard us with jealousy, though conscious of the benefits we have conferred. We have therefore to do with the *practical*. Ample supplies of books are imported from England for those natives who understand English. Are we to do nothing for the millions in the present generation, who will have no opportunity of reading these books? The Calcutta Bible Society has spent probably more than four lakhs of rupees in Bengali translations of the Scriptures, but an intelligent reading of the Scriptures requires other books explanatory, as the Bible abounds with references to subjects of Geography, Natural History, Ancient History, Jewish customs, &c. Now, these books have to be translated; and, if translations are to be condemned, it virtually amounts to condemning translations of the Scriptures, and to pronouncing useless the exertions of

Missionary societies, who in rural districts have to instruct the people through the medium of their own language. Indeed, if England itself, which possesses such a rich indigenous literature, has provided so many translations from other tongues into its own, *a fortiori*, Bengal, with its poor vernacular literature, requires translations much more urgently.

"4. It is said, that 'translations do not convey the full force of the original,'—Very true: and this is simply an argument for advising all, who can consult original works, to do so; but leading ideas and historical facts admit of being easily transferred into another tongue, and particularly into such a language as Bengali, which has such unbounded resources in compounding terms. But even in the most difficult class of works to be translated, *viz.*, the poetical, the English people insisted on having translations, as in Mickle's Lusiad, Carey's Dante, Pope's Homer, Fairfax's Tasso, Dryden's Virgil, &c. *Unless a design is entertained to extirpate the Bengali language, translations must be adopted.*"

Let us hear on this question the voice of History. We have seen lately that, the Protestant Church had been established in *Ireland* for three centuries, and hitherto has proved a signal failure in one of the objects it had in view, *viz.*, to unite England and Ireland by one religion, as well as one language—and that, after the experiment has been tried for three centuries on the part of Protestants of conveying religious knowledge solely through English, they now admit that a wrong step had been taken, and that they should have begun with education and translations into the Vernacular, as had been the practice of the Romish priesthood there. Among the *Welsh* the feeling even now is so strong, that their remonstrances succeeded in inducing the Government lately to appoint a Bishop, who could preach in Welsh. The English church has been a comparative failure in Wales, owing partly to its clergy not being acquainted with the language of the people, and despising the Vernacular. We are not advocates ourselves for perpetuating the colloquial use of the Gaelic and Welsh. We think it far better that Ireland and Wales should use the noble English language; but we adduce it to shew how difficult it is to eradicate a Vernacular language, and particularly when it is identified with the historical recollections and literary glory of a people. Queen Elizabeth proscribed under a severe penalty the use of the Irish language; and the Mussulmans applied every means to extirpate the Vernaculars of India. What have been the results, with respect to the Bengali in particular? It is increasing in richness and energy of expression every day, and is now much superior as a language, to what English was in the days of Chaucer.

In Italy, the indigenous tongue was the Latin in Roman days, the use of which has been maintained subsequently with all the influence and supremacy of the Church of Rome. All the municipal acts of the towns were recorded in Latin; public acts, solemn deeds, education, literary and scientific intercourse, all were carried on in Latin. Boccacio and Petrarch wrote their most elaborate works in Latin, despising the "lingua vulgare," the language of the mob;—(their Latin works are now forgotten, and only what they have written in the *vulgar* language *survives*). Everything, therefore, seemed to favour the perpetuation of the Latin.

But was the formation of the Italian Vernacular, which rose on the ruins of the ancient Latin, prevented? No; the influence of one man gave the impulse. Dante arose. Deeply read in classic lore, and appreciating the beauties of the Augustan age, he longed to impart them in the "lingua vulgare," and to unseal to the many what had been only known to the few: hence his immortal "Commedia," which, like Milton's Paradise Lost, will ever remain as an example of the influence of a great mind in making a language great, in wielding vulgar phrases by the magic pen of genius, and making them capable of expressing the most sublime ideas. Dante is justly called the "Father of Italian literature," as Lorenzo de Medici may be styled its foster parent, from the encouragement he gave to literary composition.

Germany comes next, where literature was at such a low ebb in the days of Frederic the Great, though Luther had ennobled and fixed the language by translating the Bible into it. Frederic the Great, not content with his military conquests, aimed at superseding German literature by French; but he succeeded as little in his efforts against the Vernacular, as the Mussalmans did in India. The moment he laid his head on the pillow of death, the German nation rose as one man in defence of their national tongue, and we see, in the prodigious strides that German literature has made since, the truth of the remark.

"Naturam fierca expelleo, tamen usque recurret."

Spain presents another strong case. The Roman and Moslem conquerors there had given every ascendancy to their languages. Yet in spite of all social and political obstacles, the Spanish language was formed and finally gained the predominance.

We hope there may be no necessity again to recur to this subject, but that all the friends of native education will co-operate on the grand basis of giving every opportunity for the attainment of a complete education both in English and the Vernacular; so as to make the former the medium for acquiring, and the latter of diffusing ideas.

—C. R., Vol. XV (1851), V—IX.

The Christian Missionaries also helped the cause of the education of Indians by the establishment of schools and colleges in this country. But what they did was from interested motives.

Missionaries and Education. The *Calcutta Review* for June, 1851, wrote :

"But it ought to be frankly acknowledged, that though the Missionaries were foremost in the field, and foremost in labour and zeal and love for the natives of this land, they do not seem to have entertained any scheme for national education, or any idea of introducing on a large scale the science and literature of Europe, as helps to Christianization, or means of social improvement." (P. 345.)

* * * *

"The great and startling success of the Hindu College attracted many eyes; and none, with greater interest, than those of the friends and supporters of Missions. It was evident that a new door of access had been opened into the native mind. The College of Serampore and Bishop's College were the first steps, on the part of the Christian community, to take advantage of the new opening; but the former was too remote, at that time, from the centre of influence; and the latter was too exclusively sectarian, and too narrow in its basis to have anything in common with a popular movement. In the meantime, while the Church of England and the Baptists were breaking ground, the Presbyterians had not been idle.

"In 1823, the Rev. Dr. Bryce memoralized the General Assembly of the Church of Scotland on the duty of sending missionaries to India—not, indeed, to teach, but to preach to the educated natives. In 1825, the Assembly agreed to establish a General Seminary of Education, with branch schools in the surrounding district, and to recommend to the head master, who was to be a regularly ordained clergyman, to give lectures, distribute fitting tracts, and use every effort to eultivate acquaintance with intelligent and educated natives.

"The Church of Scotland was even more fortunate in her choice, than the Government had been in the case of Mr. Wilson. The lustre of every other name connected with native education, pales before that of Duff; and the General Assembly's school, opened by him in 1830, soon rivalled, and speedily eclipsed the popularity of the Hindu College itself. His vast stores of information, his splendid oratorical powers, his ready and astonishing argumentative resources, the warmth and kindliness of his manner, his happy gift in teaching, of seizing the attention, and impressing the minds of the very youngest, and, above all the manifest fact. that his whole soul was in his work. in a very short time, won for him a reputation, both native and European, which has gone on increasing to this day. By sheer dint of good teaching, the school won its way into public favour. The natives forgot or sacrificed their fears and prejudices; * * " (pp. 359-60).

The Hindoo College.

"On the 20th January, 1817, the school was opened for the first time, in a house (304, Chitpore Road) hired for the purpose; * * * * * *

"During the six years that intervened between 1817 and 1823, the school was shifted about from place to place. It was first removed to another house in the Chitpore Road, then, to a house, afterwards occupied by Dr. Duff, for the General Assembly's Institution. Its next flight was of all the most eccentric. The sapient Managers removed the so-called Hindu College into the heart of the Bow Bazar; which, wher explained for the benefit of the uninitiated, means, that they took it out of the native town altogether, and set it down in a street, notorious as the haunt of drunken sailors, and the most desperate and dissolute characters of a great heathen metropolis. From this they again moved off to a scarcely more congenial vicinity—the well known Tiretta Bazar.

* * * *

"It (the Government) had already resolved to establish a Sanskrit College in 1821, and to allow

30,000 rupees annually for that purpose: and, when the question of a building for the new institution came to be entertained in 1823, happily for the Hindu College, it was agreed to locate them both under the same roof.

"'Rome,' however, 'was not built in a day.' The foundation stone of the new building was not laid, until the 25th of February, 1824; and we may notice here, that more than three years elapsed after that time ere it was ready for the reception of the students. —C. R., June, 1852, pp. 346—48.

The want of subordinates in the Medical and Public Works Departments induced the Government of India to establish Medical and Engineering Colleges in this country. The Medical College of Calcutta was established in 1835 during the regime of Lord William Bentinck. The first Indian who joined it and broke the trammels of caste prejudices by performing dissections on human bodies was the celebrated Pandit Madhu Sudan Gupta.

Regarding him, Mr. Frederick John Mouat in a lecture delivered before the Society of Arts, London, in March, 1888, said,—

"No man deserves more to live in the history of benefactors of his country than Pandit Madhu Sudan Gupta, of the Medical College of Calcutta, the first Hindu of high caste who dissected the human body in public, a feat of courage and humanity impossible to surpass, when the conditions of Hindu life are considered."

It cannot be denied that medical education was the best means of the destruction of the superstitions and prejudices of the Indian community. The establishment then of the Medical Colleges has done incalculable good to the Indian society and has been the most useful factor in the social reformation of the country. It was the students from the Medical College of Bengal who were the pioneers of Indian students in England and by their brilliant achievements in the Colleges and University of London proved to the natives of England that Indians could hold their own in every walk of life. The Indian Medical Service was the first bureaucratic fort whose strong wall wa successfully breached by the assault of a pure-blooded Indian.

The Engineering College at Rurki was established in 1847 by Mr. Thomason, Lieutenant-Governor of the North-Western Provinces, whose name it bears, for the training of subordinates required for the Ganges Canal, which was then being constructed. It has also done good work, but now it has become the stronghold not of pure-blooded natives but of "statutory" natives.

THE RENEWAL OF THE EAST INDIA COMPANY'S CHARTER IN 1853.

Up to 1853, whatever the Indian authorities did for education was in a very half-hearted and perfunctory manner. They were, to speak the truth, afraid of educating the people of this country. One Captain P. Page in his Memorandum dated East India House, April 9th, 1819, published in the Appendix to Report from Select Committee on the affairs of the East India Company, 1832, Vol. V. (Military) pp. 480-83, wrote :

"I would reward good conduct (of natives) with honour, but never with power; * * *"

"*Nullum imperium tutum, nisi benevolentia munitum.* The good will of the natives may be retained without granting them power, the semblance is sufficient; and although I abhor in private life that maxim of Rochefaucault's which recommends a man to live with his friends as if they were one day to be his enemies, I think it may be remembered with effect by the sovereigns of India."

It is possible that there were other servants of the East India Company who thought likewise and were therefore afraid of imparting education, as knowledge is power.

From the date of the attainment of political power after the battle of Plassey in 1757 down to 1853, that is, for nearly a period of 100 years, the Christian Indian authorities always discussed in all its bearings the question of the education of Indians. Was it wise and safe to educate the heathens of India?—that was the question which was often and often asked by the Christian administrators of India. Spoke Macaulay from his place in the House of Commons in 1833 :

"We shall never consent to administer the pousta to a whole community, to stupify and paralyse a great people whom God has committed to our charge, for the wretched purpose of rendering them more amenable to our control. What is power worth if it is founded on vice, on ignorance, and on misery; * * * *

"Are we to keep the people of India ignorant in order that we may keep them submissive? Or do we think that we can give them knowledge without awakening ambition? Or do we mean to awaken ambition and provide it with no legitimate vent? Who will answer one of these questions in the affirmative? Yet one of them must be answered in the affimative, by every person who maintains that we ought permanently to exclude the natives from high office. I have no fears. The path of duty is plain before us: and it is also the path of wisdom, of national prosperity, of national honour."

But an opinion has been expressed that

Macaulay was not sincere in what he said. Writes Mr. Digby in his "Prosperous British India," p. 61 :

"The climax is reached by Thomas Babington Macaulay, then Member for Leeds, who was in himself— as Law Minister in India, a Member of Parliament afterwards—to show that much of what he said was of the tongue merely and not of the heart."

The Indian authorities, it has been said, were afraid of educating the people of India.

Even so late as 1853, some of the Anglo-Indian witnesses examined before the Select Committees on Indian affairs were not in favour of educating the natives of India, for they thought that would make them disloyal. Take for instance the evidence before the Select Committee of the Commons on 4th August, 1853, of Major M. J. Rowlandson who described himself as Persian Interpreter for seventeen years under several Commanders-in-Chief at Madras and also being Secretary to a Board, and to a Committee for the public instruction of the natives of that presidency. The questions and the answers which he gave to those questions are reproduced below :

"9745. Will you state to the Committee whether you regard the operation of the Government system of education as being favourable or otherwise to the best interests of the natives of India?—The result of my experience has led me to think that it is not favorable.

* * * *

"9748. Do you or do you not regard the exclution of the Christian Scriptures, even from a class which parties might voluntarily attend in the schools supported by the Government, as a course which ought to be adopted or recommended?—I think not, from the result of my experience; and, on these grounds, that I have observed in the native pupils that while, so to speak, there was an aggravation of their capacity for evil by the elevation of their intellects, there was not a counteracting principle to prevent the exertion of that increased capacity for evil. I have seen native students who had obtained an insight into European literature and history, in whose minds there seemed to be engendered a spirit of disaffection towards the British Government.

* * * *

"9775. You have expressed an opinion that the education of the natives in India has a tendency to render them inimical to the British Government?—I believe that such is the tendency of the Government system of education.

"9776. Will you explain to the Committee what you consider to be the cause of that and what is the nature and object of their enmity to the Government? —My impression is this, that as the native of India gains an insight into the history of British India, and into the history of Europe generally, an idea is conveyed to his mind that it is something monstrous that a country like India should be possessed by a handful of foreigners; and hence, there naturally almost springs up a desire in his mind to be instrumental in setting that country free from this foreign deminance, and there being no counteracting principle, nor any sense of the duty of obedience, the natural result is a feeling of disaffection to the British Government.

"9777. Is that feeling found to exist in persons of a military class, or those who are generally supposed to be pacifically disposed?—I think I have observed it both in Mahomedans and Hindoos, particularly in Mahomedans.

"9778. Such a feeling is found to exist, notwithstanding their deep conviction of the integrity of the administration under British rule, and the mysterious character of the British power?—I think the two things exist together; one is felt by the people at large, especially by the Hindoo community, and the other I have observed in the individual instances to which I have more prominently alluded; in fact, it is the almost uniform result, as far as my experience goes, of their being enlightened *merely* in European literature.

"9779. Would not the same historical knowledge lead them to suppose that, even if they could shake off the English yoke, they would only become the subjects of military adventurers from the north, whose yoke might be still heavier?—I believe reflecting Hindoos feel that they are gainers by the rule of the British Government contrasting their present condition with what they suffered under their former Mahomedan rulers; but with native students, in the Government Schools, I repeat, one sees that the effect upon the native mind is this; there appears to be a feeling of insubordination and disquiet at the thought that they should remain under the dominion of a handful of Europeans, and from a love of change, and in the hope that in the struggle they might themselves come more to the surface, or uppermost, we find that the result is this feeling of disaffection.

"9780. Would not they be inclined to think that the result of the withdrawal of the British would be a state of anarchy?—I can quite conceive that they may think that possible; but with the hope of present advantage, and a general feeling of dislike to foreign rule, particularly when they become acquainted with the secret of the British Empire, a sense of disaffection is created, and a hope excited that in the change of masters, or in the change of rule, they may receive some personal benefit."*

This gallant officer, no doubt, represented the views and opinions of a very large class of his co-religionists and compatriots. But there were others, who did not share his views.

Thus Mr. (afterwards Sir Frederick) Halliday, who rose to be the first Lieutenant-Governor of Bengal, was asked the following question :

"8782. Is there any ground for the supposition that the spread of education is dangerous to the British Government?"

---

* Sixth Report from the Select Committee on Indian territories, 1853, pp. 155—57.

His answer was :

"None whatever; on the contrary, it appears to me that the spread of education must assist the Government. The educated classes, I think, feel themselves, and must feel themselves, more bound to us, and as having more in common with us, than they have with their uneducated countrymen, apart from the general fact that it is more easy to govern a people who have acquired a knowledge of good and evil as to government, than it is to govern them in utter ignorance; and on the whole popular knowledge is a safer thing to deal with than popular ignorance."†

The same witness mentioned how anxious the people of Bengal were to receive the benefits of English education. He said,—

"I am quite sure that the people of Bengal are in a state, ready, not only to second, but to anticipate any effort which the Government might make on the subject. The condition of Bengal, with regard to English education, is peculiar; the desire for it is becoming a craving, the people look for it most anxiously, even those of a very low class. In obscure villages, to which you could scarcely have supposed the name of English education would have reached, you find persons joining together, and making attempts to establish schools and obtain teachers, to the best of their means, and anxiously looking for assistance; at the same time doing a great deal for themselves according to the means at their disposal. It is also a

† *Ibid*, p. 59.

curious fact, that among the Bengalees, unenergetic as they are, in many respects a very extraordinary degree of energy prevails in favour of English education among those who have received it; it appears as if a reasonable inoculation of English education among them begets a strong desire to inoculate others, and to spread it to the utmost of their power. It is a very creditable point in their character. You see constantly men who have received a good education at our institutions going forth, and at great pains, and even expense, exerting themselves to the utmost for the sake of spreading knowledge, for the mere sake of the good which arises from it. It is very desirable, I think, that the Government should take speedy advantage of that extraordinary fact in the present history of the native mind in Bengal; and by doing so, I believe you might spread education enormously, and very advantageously, at a comparatively small expense."

As said so often before, the Government played a very secondary part in the dissemination of education in this country. The people themselves took the initiative and paid for their education. Could the Government now do anything to stop the flowing tide or say, "Thus far shalt thou go and no farther?" No, it was impossible for the Government to do so. Hence, they were obliged to look the danger—if imparting education to Indians were so—in the face. Yet, not in hot haste, did they take any step in the matter of the spread of education in this country. For nearly a century they discussed well this question —in all its *pros* and *cons*—before they arrived at any decision regarding it. On the occasion of the renewal of the East India Company's Charter, for the last time of its existence, in 1853, several witnesses were examined before the Parliametary Committees to give their opinions whether it was desirable to impart education to the inhabitants of India. Mr. J. C. Marshman in his evidence before the Lord's Committee on the 16th June, 1853, was asked by Lord Monteagle of Brandon :

"6566. You have given to the Committee many important recommendations, coupled with the expression of a strong opinion as to the necessity of extending education in India, and with the expression of your judgment of the inadequacy of the present resources applied for that purpose; do you apprehend any danger to British connexion in consequence of the extension of education in India?"

In reply, Mr. Marshman said,—

"I have never thought that there was any danger whatever to our political supremacy connected with the spread of education in India. I do not think that the loyalty of the natives has been in the slightest degree impaired by the amount of education which we have already communicated to them. Perhaps some of the Members of the Government may think that there is an incompatibility between the idea of a despotic Government and a free Press, and that hereafter there may possibly be some difficulties arising from the circumstances of the freedom of the Press; but even those who entertain that idea never suppose for a moment that there is any danger to our dominion from the general education of the natives."

Then he was asked by Lord Wynford—

"6567. There is no indisposition on the part of the Government of India to extend Grants for Education?"

Mr. Marshman in answer said—

"I believe that the Government of India would rejoice if they had the permission of the authorities in this country to enlarge the educational institutions; but they are of course limited by the resources at their disposal, and which can not be increased without the permission of the Home Authorities."

Sir Charles E. Trevelyan was subjected to most searching inquiry on the subject of education of Indians by the Members of the Lord's Committee on Indian Territories in 1853. His examination lasted for several days. Some of the questions put to him and his answers to them are reproduced below :

"6719. [*Chairman.*] Are the Committee to understand, that, in your opinion, the object most to be desired is to bring about a separation between India and England upon the terms most conducive to the interests of both countries, or that you think it more desirable not to bring about a separation between the two countries?

I conceive that in determining upon a line of policy we must look to the probable eventualities. We must have present to our minds what will be the ultimate result of each line of policy. Now my belief is, that *the ultimate result of the policy of improving and educating India will be, to postpone the separation for a long indefinite period*, and that when it does come, it will take place under circumstances very happy for both parties. Whereas I conceive that the result of the opposite policy of holding and governing India for the benefit of the civilians and the military men employed there, or according to any view less liberal than that of doing the utmost justice we can to India, may lead to a separation at any time, and must lead to it at a much earlier period and under much more disadvantageous circumstances than would be the result if we take the opposite course.

* * * *

"6721. Therefore, in recommending the progress of education, and, under proper safeguards, the employment of the Natives in the public service, you are not contemplating such a separation, but you are recommending a course which is, in your opinion, the least likely to lead to that alternative?

I am recommending the course which, according to my most deliberate view which I have held for a great many years, founded, I believe, on a full knowledge of the subject, will be most conducive to the continuance of our dominion, and most beneficial both to ourselves and to the Natives. I may mention, as a familiar illustration, that I was 12 years in India, and that the first six years were spent up the country, with Delhi for my headquarters, and the other six at Calcutta. The first six years represent the old regime of pure native ideas, and there were continual wars and rumours of wars. The only form which native patriotism assumed up the country was plotting against us, and meditating combinations against us and so forth. Then I came to Calcutta: and there I found quite a new state of things. The object there was to have a free Press, have Municipal institutions, to promote English education and the employment of the Natives, and various things of that sort.

"6724. Lord *Monteagle* of Brandon. Then, supposing one of two courses to be taken, either the abandonment of the education and employment of the Natives, or an extension of education, or an extension, with due precaution, of the employment of the Natives, which of those two courses, in your judgment, will lead to the longest possible continuance of the connexion of India with England?

Decidedly the extension of education and the employment of the Natives; I entertain no doubt whatever upon that question."

It is not necessary to make any further extracts from his evidence. Sir Charles Trevelyan succeeded in convincing the noble and honorable members of the Committees of both Houses of Parliament that there was not only no danger, but it would be expedient for the safety of British rule in India and maintaining the political supremacy of England in the East to educate the inhabitants of India, especially in English and to anglicise them.

Mr. Charles Hay Cameron, who was President of the Council of Education, as a witness before the Lord's Committee on the 7th July, 1853, was examined as follows :

"7450. [Lord *Monteagle* of Brandon.] Do you anticipate any danger to the connexion between England and India by the extension of education among all classes of the subjects of the Queen in India?

"No; I look upon it as a bond of union.

"7451. Will you state your reason for that opinion?

"My reason is, that their own literatures, the Sanskrit and the Mahomedan literature, are of such a character as to excite the minds of those who study them against the dominion of infidels, as the Mahomedans would say, and of Mlechas as the Hindoos would say. The influence likely to be exercised by education in our literature and science is, of course, of quite an opposite kind, calculated to inspire respect for us, as their teachers, who bring them up to the level of the most civilised nations of the world.

"7452. Would not the gravitation of the educated classes be all in the direction of the civilization of Europe, rather than the turbulence of Asia, and above all, of Asia in a state of revolution?

"I think entirely so. I think the classes we are educating know perfectly well that their sole dependence is upon us; and that if we were voluntarily to leave the country, they would immediately have to succumb to the warlike classes. They are perfectly aware of that, I think, and that their safety consists, and will consist for a great number of years to come, in the protection of the British Government.

"7459. Earl of *Ellenborough.* Do you think that we can educate the civil classes, and prevent education from reaching the military classes?

"No; I should desire to educate both.

"7454. [Lord *Monteagle* of Brandon.] Do you think that the military class, educated and improved by the course of instruction which you have witnssed in some of the Indian educational establishments, would be more dangerous to British connection than the uneducated military classes?

"No; I think it would be less dangerous, for the reason which I have given; and, looking at the examples of history, we know that the great conquering nations of antiquity educated their subjects up to their own level."

THE EDUCATION DESPATCH OF 1854.

From the evidence of competent witnesses like Marshman, Trevelyan and others before the Select Committees of the two Houses of Parliament appointed to enquire into the affairs of the East India Company on the occasion of the renewal of their Charter in 1853, the authorities were convinced that it was not politically inexpedient to educate the inhabitants of India—nay, on the contrary, the more the diffusion of education took place in India, the greater would be the security of their dominions; that educated Indians instead of being any source of danger would be towers of strength to the rulers of British India. It was after nearly a century's discussion then that the British authorities, partly, at any rate, from considerations of political expediency, determined to impart education to their Indian fellow-subjects. With that object in view was framed the famous Educational Despatch of 1854, commonly known as "the Intellectual Charter of India" or as Wood's Despatch, for Sir Charles Wood was then President of the Board of Control of the East India Company, a situation corresponding at present to that of the Secretary of

State for India. This document is attributed to the pen of Mr. John Stuart Mill, the well-known English thinker and philosopher, who was at that time a clerk in the India Office. But we think we are right in saying that it was prepared by Lord Northbrook.

The Education Despatch of 1854 was a feeble imitation of the English Education Minute of 1853. Regarding this Minute, Frof. Holman writes that

"On April 2, 1853, appeared the great revolutionary minute, ...

"This was indeed a far-reaching act. At last the education of the people is very definitely, though by no means wholly, in the hands of the government. At least they are going to provide, more or less effectively, for the doing of the work; though the initiation and control of this work is left in the hands of private individuals, acting under certain limitations and obligations imposed by the Committee of Council." (*Loc. Cit.* pp. 128-30).

This despatch consisted of a hundred paragraphs and was addressed by the Court of Directors of the East India Company to the Governor-General of India in Council, dated 19th July, 1854, No. 49. The opening paragraphs breathe lofty philanthropy and altruism;—

1. "It appears to us that the present time, when by an Act of the Imperial Legislature the responsible

trust of the Government of India has again been placed in our hands, is peculiarly suitable for the review of the progress which has already been made, the supply of existing deficiencies, and the adoption of such improvements as may be best calculated to secure the ultimate benefit of the people committed to our charge.

2. "Among many subjects of importance, none can have a stronger claim to our attention than that of education. It is one of our most sacred duties to be the means, as far as in us lies, of conferring upon the natives of India those vast moral and material blessings which flow from the general diffusion of useful knowledge, and which India may, under Providence, derive from her connection with England. For, although British iufluence has already, in many remarkable instances, been applied with great energy and success to uproot demoralising practices, and even crimes of a deeper dye, which for ages had prevailed among the natives of India, the good results of those efforts must, in order to be permanent, possess the further sanction of a general sympathy in the native mind, which the advance of education alone can secure."

The concluding paragraphs of the Despatch ran as follows:

"As a Government, we can do no more than direct the efforts of the people, and aid them wherever they appear to require most assistance. The result depends more upon them than upon us; and although we are fully aware that the measures we have now adopted will involve in the end a much larger expenditure upon education from the revenues of India, or, in other words, from the taxation of the people of India, than is at present so applied, we are convinced, with Sir Thomas Munro, in words used many years since, that any expense which may be incurred for this object, 'will be amply repaid by the improvement of the country; for the general diffusion of knowledge is inseparably followed by more orderly habits, by increasing industry, by a taste for the comforts of life, by exertion to acquire them, and by the growing prosperity of the people'."

Regarding this Despatch, which was reprinted by the General Council of Education in India, in a note to the reprint, the Secretary of that Council, the Rev. James Johnston, wrote :

"This important despatch, which was sent out to the Indian Government 1854, by Sir Charles Wood (Viscount Halifax), then President of the Board of Control, and was ratified, after the mutiny, by the despatch of Lord Stanley (Earl of Derby) in 1859, is still the great Charter of Education in India.

"It is reprinted by the 'General Council of Education in India,' for the purpose of showing how admirably it is fitted to meet the great want of that country—a healthful and liberal education. *Their only regret is, that its rules have been so little applied to the general education of the poor, for which it was specially designed; and that its principles have been and still are, so largely departed from in regard to the higher education.* And their great aim is, to press upon Government, both at home and in India, the importance of seeing to the faithful and adequate carrying out of its provisions."

The Educational Department as it exists in this country at present has been the outcome of that Despatch. The Educational Department seemed to have been designed, among other reasons, for making provision for natives of England. Englishmen were (and are now)* appointed to all the high and coveted posts in the service.

But the education of Indians was also a necessity, for otherwise it was impossible for the Indian Government to secure public servants to fill the subordinate posts in the State. This is evident from the Educational Despatch itself. Thus in its third paragraph, it is written :

"We have, moreover, always looked upon the encouragement of education as peculiarly important, because calculated 'not only to produce a higher degree of intellectual fitness, but to raise the moral character of those who partake of its advantages, and so *to supply you with servants* to whose probity you may with increased confidence commit offices of trust'," &c.

---

* The case is worse now than formerly, since the establishment of the Indian Educational Service, which is called Indian, perhaps because it is practically closed against Indians, that is, natives of India. In reply to the Hon. Mr. B. N. Basu's interpellation in the Imperial Legislative Council, it was stated that there are 208 Europeans against 3 Indians in the Indian Educational Service. [Written in 1912.]

*   *   *   *

Also in the 72nd paragraph they wrote :

"We have always been of opinion that the spread of education in India will produce a greater efficiency in all branches of administration, by enabling you to obtain the services of intelligent and trustworthy persons in every department of Government; * * *"

Again in the 73rd paragraph of the Despatch, they wrote;—

"And we understand that it is often not so much the want of Government employment as *the want of properly qualified persons to be employed by Government, which is felt, at the present time, in many parts of India.*"

In the next paragraph (74), the reason of educated men not accepting Government employment was mentioned. It was there stated,—

"And we can readily believe, with the Secretary to the Board of Revenue in Bengal, that young men who have passed a difficult examination in the highest branches of philosophy and mathematics, are naturally disinclined to accept such employment as persons who intend to make the public service their profession must necessarily commence with."

They also did not lose sight of other advantages that would result to England from the education of Indians. This would

"secure to us a larger and more certain supply of many articles necessary for our manufactures and extentively consumed by all classes of our population, as well as an almost inexhaustible demand for the produce of British labour."*

It was not, therefore, entirely from motives of pure philanthropy that education was sought to be imparted to Indians and the Despatch was prepared. The Despatch itself clearly indicates philanthropy, political expediency, administrative necessity and commercial expansion as the motives. In fact it is only children, old or young, who believe in unmixed generosity as the motive of any public measure in any country, Western or Eastern, which has a governing class or caste. In such countries one of the motives is always political expediency or administrative necessity. And this is not necessarily a sinister motive, though it is not philanthropy.

The Government of India also did not act upon all the suggestions and recommendations laid down in the Educational Despatch. Lord Dalhousie was the Governor-General of India to whom the Despatch was addressed. It fell to his lot to organise the Educational Department. His latest biographer Sir William Lee Warner says that he had to carry out the policy dictated to him by the home authorities, that is to say, Dalhousie was acting upon what another Scotch

* Paragraph 4 of the Despatch.

Governor-General, Lord Elgin, called the "Mandate Theory."

It did not suit the convenience of the East India Company to do anything for the technical education of Indians. England never did anything for India which in any way came in conflict with her interests, or which would not make India depend on her for her material welfare. So while in England grants of money were made to Mechanics' Institutes, for the encouragement of art instruction, nothing of the sort was done in India. Prof. Holman writes that

"In 1841 Mr. Gillon moved, in the Commons, that grants of money be made to Mechanics' Institutes, for the encouragement of art instruction other than that given in schools of design. Sir Robert Peel supported the motion, on the grounds that foreign countries, especially Prussia, were in advance of us in art instruction, and, therefore, our industries would be likely to suffer; also such work as was done in Mechanics' Institutes was good for the health and morals of the working-classes." (*Loc. Cit.* p. 80).

Sir Charles E. Trevelyan in his evidence before the Select Committee of the House of Lords on the Government of India Territories, on 21st June, 1853, pleaded in very strong terms for the technical education of Indians. In answer to a question of the Earl of Ellenborough, he said :

"I would also establish a college for instruction in art. The natives have great capacities for art. They have a remarkable delicacy of touch; they have great accuracy of eye; and their power of imitation is quite extraordinary. The extent to which they are capable of successfully cultivating the decorative and fine arts has been shown by the result of the recent Exhibition in London. I beg leave to read two or three extracts from reports upon the Great Exhibition, which will establish that point. This is a report from Mr. Owen Jones upon the decorative arts in connection with the Exhibition:—'In the East Indian Collection of textile fabrics at the Great Exhibition, the perfection at which their artists have arrived is most marvellous; it was hardly possible to find a discord; contrasting colours appeared to have just the tone and shade required. The contrivances by which they corrected the power of any one colour in excess were most ingenious.' * * * * 'It would be very desirable that we should be made acquainted with the manner in which, in the education of the Eastern artists, the management of colour is made so perfect. It is most probable that they work only from tradition, and a highly endowed natural instinct for which all Eastern nations have ever been remarkable.' In another paper, Mr. Owen Jones says, 'In the Indian Collection, we find no struggle after an effect; every ornament arises quietly and naturally from the object decorated, inspired by some true feeling, or embellishing some real want; the same guiding principle, the same evidence of thought and feeling in the artist is everywhere present, in the embroidered and woven garment tissues as in the humblest earthen vase, * * * * 'In the management of colour, again, the Indians, in common with most Eastern nations, are very perfect; we see here the most brilliant colours harmonised as by a natural instinct —it is difficult to find a discord; the relative values of the colours of ground and surfaces are most admirably felt.' * * * * And, 'The temporary exhibition of the Indian and other Eastern Collections in the Great Exhibition of 1851, was a boon to all those European artists who had an opportunity of studying them; and let us trust that the foresight of the Government, which has secured to us a portion of those collections as permanent objects of study, will lead to still higher results.

"Mr. Waagen, the Superintendent of the National Gallery at Berlin, and a well-known writer upon art, says, 'In the fabrics of India, the correct principle that patterns and colours should diversify plain surfaces, without destroying or disturbing the impression of flatness, is as carefully observed as it was in the middle ages, when the decoration of walls, pavements and carpets was brought to such perfection by the Arabs. But it is not only the observance of this principle which distinguishes the Indian stuffs in the Exhibition, they are remarkable for the rich inventions shown in the patterns, in which the beauty, distinction and variety of the forms, and the harmonious blending of severe colours, called forth the admiration of all true judges of art. What a lesson such designs afford to manufacturers, even in those nations in Europe which have made the greatest progress in industry.'

"The last extract I will give is the following, from

Mr. Redgrave's work on Design:—' If we look at the details of the Indian patterns, we shall be surprised at their extreme simplicity, and be led to wonder at their rich and satisfactory effect. It will soon be evident, however, that their beauty results entirely from adherence to the principles above described. The parts themselves are often poor, ill-drawn and common-place; yet, from the knowledge of the designer, due attention to the just ornamentation of the fabric, and the refined delicacy evident in the selection of *quantity* and the choice of tints, both for the ground, where gold is not used as a ground, and for the ornamental forms, the fabrics, individually and as a whole, are a lesson to our designers and manufacturers, given by those from whom we least expected it. Moreover, in the adaptation of all these qualities of design to the fabrics for which they are intended, there is an entire appreciation of the effects to be produced by the texture and foldings of the tissue when in use as an article of dress, in so much that no draft of the design can be made in any way to show the full beauty of the manufactured article, since this is only called out by the motion and folding on the fabric itself. An expression of admiration for these manufactures must be called forth from every one who examines them, and is justly due to merits which are wholly derived from the true principles on which these goods have been ornamented, and which result from perfect consistency in the designer.' "

" 6636. Earl of *Ellenborough.*] Were you not disappointed by the Indian part of the exhibition; did you think it a fair representative of India?

"No; such as it was, it excited the admiration of people here, but it was decidedly inferior to what may be seen in India. Those who have seen the beautiful buildings designed and erected by the natives at Agra, Delhi, Beejapore and Mandoo, will say at once that what appeared at the exhibition was a very inadequate representation of what they are capable of."

"6637. *Chairman.*] That being your opinion, how would you set about instituting such a department?

"I would make the institution in Jermyn-Street the model for the College of Science, and the institution at Marlborough-House the model for the College of Art. Art is taught there systematically, * * * * I would establish an institution at Calcutta on that model. I *conceive that there is a peculiar call upon us to give the natives of India all the advantage in the cultivation of the arts which it is in our power to give; for in order to favour our manufactures, we have, partly by levying no duty upon English manufactures imported into India, and partly by levying a heavy duty upon Indian manufactures imported into England, in addition to the natural manufacturing superiority of England, by these means swept away great branches of manufacture, and have caused great distress in India: consequently, I consider that we owe a heavy debt to India in this respect, and that it is specially our duty to give to our Indian fellow-subjects every possible aid in cultivating those branches of art that still remain to them;* and I consider that in doing so, we shall benefit ourselves as much as them, and that an institution such as I have described, in which the results of Indian art would be displayed for the imitation of the world, would be quite as important in its relation to European art as it would be in its relation to Native art.

"6638. Lord *Monteagle.*] Was not there at one time a heavier duty in India itself upon cottons manufactured in India than upon cottons exported from England?

"Yes; from the renewal of the Charter in 1813, until the Transit Duties were abolished, English Cotton Goods were charged only 2½, while the aggregate of the duties leyied upon Native Cotton Goods was 17½ per cent. * *."

"6639. Were not India cottons paying 17½ per cent. duty in India, while the English were paying 5 per cent.?

"English cottons paid only 2½ per cent. on their importation into India. *It was a great injustice that heavy duties were levied upon the cottons of India in India; and that another heavy duty was levied upon them when imported into England.* * * * *"

"6640. Earl of *Ellenborough.*] Is it not calculated that in addition to the returns from India, for what is exported to India, India has to remit to this country large sums every year, to the amount of nearly a million and a half?

"Much more than that; I think exceeding three millions for the Government only, besides all the private remittances. If we take the Government remittances at three millions, and private remittances at half that, we have the sum of four millions and a half to be remitted every year from India to England, which forms a great incubus upon the Indian trade. * * *"

But the pleading of Sir Ch. Trevelyan for the technical education of Indians was fruitless.

FEMALE EDUCATION WAS NOT ENCOURAGED BY THE EAST INDIA COMPANY.

No portion of the sum of one lac of rupees allotted for the education of natives was to be spent on female education. It was left to the people to provide for the education of the fair sex of their country. What they did in Bengal for female education has been told by a writer in the pages of the *Calcutta Review* for July, 1855, as follows :

" It was somewhere about 1818 or 1819, that a Society, called, we believe, the Union School Society, was formed in Calcutta, for educational purposes. Shortly after its formation, its members, encouraged by the success that had attended their operations amongst the boys, determined to make an attempt in the direction of female education. At the invitation of this Society Miss Cooke came to Calcutta, having been selected for this most difficult service, if we have been rightly informed, and our memory serve us aright, by the celebrated Richard Cecil, whose admirable sagacity was never more distinctly manifested than in this selection. Miss Cooke arrived in Calcutta in May, 1821, * * We have stated that she came on the invitation of a certain educational society; but on her arrival, it appeared that the native members of the Committee of that Society, although they had spoken well while yet the matter was at a distance and in the region of theory, recoiled from the obloquy of so rude an assault on time-honored custom. * * * *

"The babus had been brought up to the talking-point, but not to the acting-point. An arrangement was however entered into with the Church Mission Society, and Miss Cooke began her operations under their auspices. An account of the commencement of these operations is given by Mrs. Chapman, in her little work on Female Education; and we are sure that we shall gratify our readers by extracting it at length—

"'Whilst engaged in studying the Bengali language, and scarcely daring to hope that an immediate opening for entering upon the work, to which she had devoted herself, would be found, Miss Cooke paid a visit to one of the native schools for boys, in order to observe their pronunciation; and this circumstance, trifling as it may appear, led to the opening of her first school in Thunthuniya. Unaccustomed to see a European lady in that part of the native town a crowd collected round the door of the school. Amongst them was an interesting looking girl, whom the school pundit drove away. Miss Cooke desired the child to be called, and by an interpreter asked her if she wished to learn to read. She was told in reply, that this child had for three months past been daily begging to learn to read with the boys, and that if Miss Cooke (who had made known her purpose of devoting herself to the instruction of native girls) would attend next day, twenty girls should be collected. Accompanied by a female friend, conversant with the language, she repeated her visit on the morrow and found fifteen girls, several of whom had their mothers with them. Their natural inquisitiveness prompted them to enquire what could be Miss Cooke's motive for coming amongst them. They were told that she had heard in England, that the women of their country were kept in total ignorance, that they were not taught to read or write, that the men only were allowed to attain any degree of knowledge, and it was also generally understood that the chief obstacle to their improvement was that no females would undertake to teach them; she had therefore felt compassion for them, and had left her country, her parents and friends, to help them. The mothers with one voice cried out, smiting themselves with their right hands, "Oh what a pearl of a woman is this!" It was added, she has given up every earthly expectation, to come here, and seeks not the riches of the world, but desires only to promote your best interests.'—'Our children are yours, we give them to you.' 'What will be the use of learning to our girls, and what good will it do to them?' She was told;—'It will make them more useful in their families, and increase their knowledge, and it was hoped that it would also tend to give them respect, and produce harmony in their families'—'True (said one of them) our husbands now look upon us as little better than brutes.' Another asked, 'What benefit will you derive from this work!' She was told that the only return wished for, was to promote their best interest and happiness. Then said the woman, 'I suppose this is a holy work, and well-pleasing to God.' As they were not able to understand much, it was only said in return that God was always well-pleased that his servants should do good to their fellow-creatures. The women then spoke to each other, in terms of the highest approbation, of what had passed."

* * * *

"In the course of the first year eight schools were established, attended, more or less regularly, by 214 girls.

"Two or three years after Miss Cooke's arrival in India, she became the wife of the Rev. Issac Wilson, a Missionary of the Church Mission Society; but she did not relax in her efforts in behalf of the good cause * * * * Mrs. Wilson's efforts were now directed to the obtaining of the means of erecting a suitable building for a Central School. In order to do this, it was found necessary to establish a special Society for Native Female Education. This Society was established in the beginning of 1824. Funds were raised, and on the 18th of May, 1826, the foundation stone of the Central School, in Cornwallis Square, was laid. In connection with this building, we must not omit to notice the extraordinary munificence of a native gentleman, the Rajah Buddinath Roy, who subscribed the very large sum of 20,000 Sicca Rupees, or upwards of £2,000 sterling, towards the erection. We believe this donation for a great patriotic object, is to this day unrivalled in the annals of native liberality; and it is properly commemorated by the following inscription on a marbel tablet, inserted into the wall of the principal hall in the institution;—

This
Central School,
Founded by a Society of Ladies,
For the Education of
Native Female Children,
was greatly assisted by
A liberal donation of Rs. 20,000, from
RAJAH BUDDINATH ROY BAHADUR;
and its objects further promoted
and funds saved by
Charles Knowles Robinson, Esq.,
Who planned and executed this building,
1828.

"* * * * On the 1st April, 1828, she removed into the new building in Cornwallis Square, and into that focus the rays of her influence, which had been before so widely diffused, were now concentrated."

In ancient India, and even before the British occupation of this country, the womenfolk of India as a class were not altogether illiterate. But up to 1853, the Indian Government did not do anything for female education. It was not encouraged, because from the utilitarian point of view, it was of little use to Government. Women clerks and women subordinate officials were not in demand then in Government establishments and hence there was no need for educated females. And so they tried to find reasons for not educating Indian women. Thus the Lord Bishop of Oxford asked Sir Charles Trevelyan who appeared as a witness before the Lords' Committee on the Government of Indian territories on 28th June, 1853 :

"6818. Can you state to the Committee whether one of the objections to the education of females in India is not the fact, that they must, if they study oriental literature at all, study books of this exceedingly debasing character?

"It is very unusual for females to cultivate the learned languages; * * * * I presume the question does not relate to their studying the learned languages; and as regards the vernacular languages, it depends entirely upon the guidance under which they are. If they are under the guidance of Missionaries or good Christian people or even of enlightened moral Hindus and Mahomedans, there is now a sufficient body of vernacular literature of an improving and elevating character to furnish the basis of a system of instruction for them, and it is rapidly increasing.

"6819. But my question is not whether they could not be taught in something else; but whether you are cognizant of the fact, that one of the great objections to be made against females studying these languages was the necessity, if they studied the learned languages at all, of their being made conversant with a particular kind which even male Hindoos thought unfit for females?

"I never before heard it even proposed that native females should study the learned languages of India; but certainly from my knowledge of those languages,

I should say that it would be impossible for a female to cultivate Sanskrit literature without learning a great deal which would be extremely objectionable for any female to read.

"6820. Even in the estimate of a Hindoo?

"Yes, even in the estimate of a Hindoo, because, whatever license they may take themselves, they are very careful of the purity of their women.

"6821. Lord *Monteagle* of Brandon.] The Committee are aware that the late Mr. Bethune, with great generosity, devoted the sum of £10,000 for female education; and I believe other persons of piety and earnestness in India have looked with great anxiety to the education of native females. Is there any instance that has ever come to your knowledge of the female instruction so established, or so contemplated, involving that which has formed the subject of the questions that have been recently put to you, namely, the cultivation of the ancient learned languages?

"Never. The idea is quite new to me.

"6822. You never heard of that either in Asia or in England?

"Never. * * It is, however, evident from the Sanskrit Plays, that in very ancient times, women of rank, at least, were taught to read and write, and the accomplishments of drawing and music. Urvasi extemporises a verse which she writes upon a birch leaf, and which, falling into the hands of the Queen of Pururavas, is read by her principal female attendant. Malati draws a picture of her beloved Madhava; and frequent allusions are made to the Sangita Sala, or Music Hall. In the Ajunta Cave paintings, women are represented as engaged in study with books of palm-leaves.

"6823. Lord Bishop of *Oxford.*] Is it not the fact, that it is a principle settled in the Native mind, that females should not be educated?.

"I do not recollect any precept to that effect in their books. * * * *

"6824. My question was, not what the sacred books of the Hindoos taught, but whether there was not in the Native mind, generally, a settled feeling against the education of their females?

"Yes, I think there is a very strong prejudice against it; I do not think it goes the length of a principle: * *

"6825. There is a strong prejudice in the native mind against the instruction and education of females?

"Undoubtedly.

"6826. That is not of recent date, is it?

"No, ancient date; it is gradually yielding to the progress of enlightenment; * *

"6825. You have stated to the Committee, that there has been of long standing a strong and great prejudice in the native mind against the instruction of their females; during the whole time that that prejudice has been growing up, was it not impossible that any one of their females should become learned in their literature without becoming conversant with those abominations which it contains?

"There are degrees; but, speaking generally, that was the case certainly.

"6828. To be conversant with those abominations

would even, according to Hindoo notions, be unfit for females?

" If it had seriously entered into the contemplation of a Hindoo to teach his wife or daughters Sanskrit, I have no doubt that objection would have occurred to him.

" 6829. Therefore, in fact, it was impossible that there could be any teaching of females without making them acquainted with that against which the native mind itself would have revolted?

" Yes.

" 6830. May we not, in looking back to the long period through which this state of things has lasted, see one reason for the peculiarly strong prejudice in the native against female education in that fact?

" I think so.

" 6831. If that is the case, is it not exceedingly important, if we wish to break down that prejudice, that we should set the example of educating the men in a literature which would not necessarily bring them into contact with such abominations?

" Certainly.

" 6832. Earl of *Harrowby*.] An Indian Female could not make any progress in Native literature without passing through the study of very corrupt books?

" With the exception of the nascent vernacular literature, which is principally supported by the Missionaries.

" 6833. Do you believe that the feeling of hostility to female education which exists in the Hindoo mind arises from the nature of their literature, or from the general notion existing amongst all those nations, that the women ought to occupy a subordinate conditions?

"I think that the primary and main reason is, that in order to keep the women in subjection and seclusion, it is necessary to keep them ignorant. It arises from the same cause which induces them to keep their women in seclusion; but, no doubt if there were not that reason, the other would be a sufficient one.

"6834. And, therefore, that would be an obstacle to any future progress in female education, unless a literature of a better kind was supplied?

"Yes."

"6835. Lord Bishop of *Oxford*.] A literature of a better kind, which shall be employed as an instrument of male progress?

"Yes."

Of course, it was prejudice against every thing Indian which dictated the above questions and their answers. Sanskrit is not so *rich* in books of an exceedingly debasing character as the classical languages of Europe. Sir Richard Burton, when he translated the *Arabian Nights* into English, was told that he probably would be prosecuted for publishing his translation because it abounded with many obscene and abominable passages and incidents. His reply was very characteristic. He said that he would go to the Court before which he was to be prosecuted armed with the Bible in one hand and Shakespeare's works in the other. He did not consider the *Arabian Nights* more abominale or obscene than the Sacred Scriptures of the Christians or the plays of the greatest dramatist of the English. It cannot be said that there was not a substratum of truth in his contention. If English women can read the Bible and Shakespeare, unexpurgated, without getting their morals corrupted, there is no reason why Indian ladies should not be instructed in Sanskrit.

Although the Educational Despatch recommended the encouragement of Female Education, the Indian Government did not do all that they ought to have done for it. The initiative was not taken by the Government in female education. It was, as in the case of the higher education of males, taken in hand by private individuals, most notable among whom was Mr. Drinkwater Bethune. He was a great friend of Dr. Frederick John Mouat, who in a lecture delivered before the Society of Arts, London, in March, 1888, said :

"Two days before the close of his honoured and valued life Mr. Bethune, at whose beside I was watching and whose eyes I closed in their eternal sleep, asked me how long he had to live. 'Don't conceal it from me,' he said, 'as I wish to complete the last work of my life.' When I mentioned to him that I could only measure it by hours, he called for his cheque book, drew a cheque for a very large amount and bid me hasten until he had passed away, for the benefit of the female school he had established. This was done. I was his executor and found that the whole of his large official income in India was spent in the country and chiefly in good works of which the foundation of the female school which bears his name, was the chief."

We need not dwell at any great length on the Education Despatch of 1854. We have said enough to show the motives which led the authorities to prepare it, and also how and why the recommendations contained in it were not given effect to by the Government of the East India Company.

THE ESTABLISHMENT OF THE PRESIDENCY UNIVERSITIES.

Dr. Frederick John Mouat came out to India in the service of the East India Company as an Assistant Surgeon on the Bengal Establishment in the year 1840. He succeeded Mr. David Hare as Secretary of the Calcutta Medical College and was also placed on the professorial staff of that Institution. It was due to his exertions that the buildings of the Calcutta Medical College and the hospital attached to it were erected. Again it was due to his advice and exhortations that the four Bengalee Medical students, the well known Dr. Bhola Nath Bose and Dr. Surya Kumar Goodeeve Chuckerbutty and two others, went to England in 1844 to complete their education.

Dr. Mouat was also appointed Secretary of the Council of Education. In those days there was no Director of Public Instruction or any Inspector of Schools under him. The duties of both these posts had to be discharged by the Secretary of the Council. So Dr. Mouat had to inspect all the schools and colleges in the province of Bengal affiliated to the Council of Education. As a result of his inspections, he conceived the ideas of the establishment of a University for Bengal. In a lecture delivered by him on the 23rd March, 1888 before the Society of Arts of London, he said :

"When I joined therefore and had personally visited all the colleges and schools under the charge of the Council and had become acquainted with the standards in use, I was at once struck with the absence of any definite aim and object in the system of education adopted in all. It appeared to me that a great scheme of public instruction worked by an able staff and turning out annually numerous schools of considerable merits and attainments needed some means of acknowledgment of the position they ought to occupy as men of culture and education. I rapidly arrived at the conclusion that nothing short of a university having the power to grant degrees would accomplish this purpose.

"I accordingly placed myself at once in communication with my friend Professor Malden of University College in London. From the information which I placed before him, Professor Malden considered Bengal to be perfectly ready for the establishment of Universities and sent me a copy of the history of those institutions in Europe written by himself. I then conferred with the President Mr. Charles Hay Cameron on the subject, told him what I had done, &c., &c. I was directed to prepare the scheme, which I did accordingly," &c.

His scheme was that the University in

Bengal should be established on the model of that of London. He said :

> "After carefully studying the laws and constitution of the Universities of Oxford and Cambridge with those of the recently established University of London, the latter alone appears adapted to me to the wants of the native community."

His proposed plan of the University of Calcutta is given in full as Appendix O to the Second Report of the Select Committee of the House of Lords on the Government of Indian Territories, 1853.

Dr. Mouat's plan was submitted through the Government of India to the authorities of the East India Company by whom, of course, it was not approved of. They were averse to the extension of education among Indians and so they naturally put their foot on Dr. Mouat's scheme. It was on the eve of the renewal of the East India Company's Charter that Mr. Cameron submitted a petition dated 30th November, 1852, to the House of Lords in which he showed the causes which operated as hindrances to the spread of education among Indians. He wrote :

> "That, as President of the Council of Education for Bengal, your petitioner had opportunities of observing the desire and the capacity of large numbers of the native youth of India for the acquisition of European

literature and science, as well as the capacity of the most distinguished among them for fitting themselves to enter the Civil and Medical covenanted services of the East India Company, and to practise in the learned professions.

"That the said native youths are hindered from making all the progress they are capable of in the acquisition of the said literature and science:

"1st. Because there is not in British India any University with power to grant degrees, as is done by Universities in Europe.

"2ndly. Because the European instructors of the said native youths do not belong to any of the covenanted services of the East India Company, and do not, therefore, whatever may be their learning and talents, occupy a position in Society which commands the respect of their pupils.

"3rdly. Because no provision has been made for the education of any of the said native youth in England without prejudice to their caste or religious feelings.

"Your petitioner therefore prays,

"That one or more universities may be established in British India.

"That a covenanted education service may be created, analogous to the covenanted civil and medical services.

"That one or more establishments may be created, at which the native youth of India may receive, in England, without prejudice to their caste or religious feelings, such a secular education as may qualify them for admission into the civil and medical services of the East India Company."

Regarding this petition and his prayer for the establishment of one or more Universities in British India, Mr. Cameron was very searchingly examined on the 7th July, 1853 by the Lords' Committee on the Government of Indian territories.

"7316. *Chairman.*] In a petition which has been presented to the House of Lords from you, in that portion of it which relates to education, your first prayer is that one or more Universities may be established in British India; will you be so good as to state to the Committee somewhat more in detail what your suggestion will amount to?

"My suggestion would amount to this, that there should be in each of the great capital cities in India a University; that is to say, at Calcutta, at Madras, at Bombay and at Agra; those four cities being the centres of four distinct languages; Calcutta being the focus of the Bengalee language; Madras of the Tamil, Bombay of the Mahrattee, and Agra of the Hindee. In those four Universities would be taught, according to my notions, the English language and all the literature that it contains; and science also in the same language; and at the same time the four languages that I have mentioned would also be cultivated. Native students would be practised in translations from English into each of those languages, and from each of those languages into English. Every encouragement which the Government can give would be given to the production of original works in those Native languages. That system already exists to a considerable extent;

but there is no University; there is no body which has the power of granting degrees; and that sort of encouragement appears to be one which the Natives are fully desirous of. They have arrived at a point at which they are quite ripe for it, and they themselves are extremely desirous of it: that is to say, those who have already benefited by this system of English education are extremely desirous of those distinctions, and are extremely desirous of having that sort of recognition of their position as subjects of the Queen of Great Britain.

"7317. Would you assimilate the degrees to the degrees conferred at the London University?

"The plan that we suggested when I was President of the Council of Education, * * * was founded upon the plan of the London University; we copied it *mutatis mutandis* from that plan.

* * * *

"7322. Would that, in your opinion, improve the general tone and character of the education given throughout India?

"I should think very much so indeed.

* * * *

"7325. Earl of *Ellenborough.*] Would you give the same titles as in England of Master of Arts and Bachelor of Arts; do not you think they would like "Bahadur" and "Rajah" rather better?

"I think they would like to be admitted into the Enropean republic of letters better than to have those natives titles to which your Lordship alludes."

It is not necessary to make further extracts from the Evidence of Mr. Cameron. The Parliamentary Committees after all must have been convinced that there was no harm in establishing one or more universities in India.

So the Directors of the East India Company were after all persuaded to recommend the establishment of Universities in India on the model of the University of London. In their Educational Despatch of 1854, they wrote :

"Some years ago, we declined to accede to a proposal made by the Council of Education and transmitted to us, with the recommendation of your Government, for the institution of an university in Calcutta. The rapid spread of a liberal education among the Natives of India since that time, the high attainments shown by the Native Candidates for Government Scholarships, and by Native students in private institutions, the success of the Medical Colleges, and the requirements of an increasing European and Anglo-Indian population, have led us to the conclusion that the time has now arrived for the establishment of universities in India, which may encourage a regular and liberal course of education, by conferring academical degrees as evidences of attainment in the different branches of art and science, and by adding marks of honour for those who may desire to compete for honorary distinction.

"The Council of Education, in the proposal to which we have alluded, took the London University as their model; and we agree with them, that the form, government, and functions of that university * * * are the best adapted to the wants of India, and may be followed with advantage, although some variation will be necessary in points of detail."

* * * *

"We desire that you take into your consideration the Institution of Universities at Calcutta and Bombay, upon the general principles which we have now explained to you, and report to us upon the best method of procedure, with a view to their incorporation by Acts of the Legislative Council of India.

* * * *

"We shall be ready to sanction the creation of an university at Madras, or in any other part of India, where a sufficient number of institutions exist from which properly qualified candidates for degrees could be supplied; it being in our opinion advisable that the great centres of European Government and civilization in India should possess universities similar in character to those which will now be founded, as soon as the extension of a liberal education shows that their establishment would be of advantage to the Native communities."

But the Government of India were not in a hurry to give effect to the recommendation of the Court of Directors of the East India Company and establish Universities. These were not established during the Governor-Generalship of Lord Dalhousie, the Scotch "Laird of Cockpen,"* but of his successor Lord Canning. It was in the year 1857, the year of the outbreak of the Indian Mutiny and the last year of the existence of the East India Company, that the Legislative Act was passed sanctioning the establishment of the Universities at Calcutta, Bombay and Madras.

CONVERSION AND EDUCATION OF INDIANS

The Situation in 1813.

In the Charter Act of 1813, to promote the happiness of the heathens of India, it was proposed that

"Such measures ought to be adopted as may tend to the introduction among them of useful knowledge, and of religious and moral improvement; and in furtherance of the above objects, sufficient facilities ought to be afforded by law to persons desirous of going to and remaining in India, for the purpose of accomplishing those benevolent designs." * *

Before proceeding further, it is necessary to point out the diplomatic language of the above clause of the Charter Act. It is language befitting a Machiavelli or a Talleyrand—which does not so much express as conceal the thoughts and objects which the framers of the Act had in view. Who are the persons referred to as "desirous of going to and remaining in India, for the purpose of accomplishing those benevolent designs?" They were Christian missionaries.

It should be remembered that in England,

"In former times education was, for the most part, of the church, by the church, and for the church; and it was only as the advantage, or necessity, of extending it to the laity, for the purpose of confirming and expanding the influence and authority of the church, was realized, that knowledge was more generally imparted."*

At the time of the East India Company's charter of 1813, education in England was still under the control of the Church. Hence, the framers of the charter could not think of imparting education to Indians without ecclesiastical agency. This explains the diplomatic language of the Charter.

It would have been outraging the feelings of Indians to have informed them of the Ecclesiastical Department that they were going to be saddled with, for the benefit of the Christian natives of England. Hence the diplomatic language of the Charter Act. Christian missionaries were not required in India—they were not for the benefit of the heathens of that land. The witnesses examined before the Committees of the two Houses were mostly opposed to the sending of them to India. Mr. Warren Hastings was asked by the Lords' Committee :

" Would the introduction of a Church establishment into the British territories in the East Indies, probably be attended with any consequences which would be injurious to the stability of the Government of India?"

* English National Education by H. Holman, London, 1898, p. 12.

In reply, he said :

"I have understood that a great fermentation has arisen in the minds of the natives of India who are subject to the authority of the British Government, and that not partial, but extending to all our possessions, arising from a belief, however propagated, that there was an intention in this Government to encroach on the religious rights of the people. From the information of persons who have recently come from the different establishments of India, Your Lordships will easily know whether such apprehensions still subsisted when they left it, or whether the report of them is groundless; but if such apprehensions do exist, everything that the irritable minds of the people can connect with that will make an impression upon them, which they will adopt as certain assurances of it. So far only, considering the question as a political one, I may venture to express my apprehension of the consequences of such establishment at this particular season; in no other light am I permitted to view it." * *

In answering the question.

"Do you conceive that any attempts to introduce the Christian religion among the natives would be attended with dangerous political consequences?"

Sir John Malcolm told the Lords' Committee:

"With the most perfect conviction upon my mind, that, speaking humanly, the Christian religion has been the greatest blessing that could be bestowed on mankind, * * * nothing but the strongest impression of the danger that would attend, not merely the attempt, but an impression among the inhabitants of India that such as attempt would be made, could lead me to give a decided opinion that it would be attended with the most dangerous consequences; and I think the risk of those dangers would be encountered without the slightest prospect of accomplishing the object; my reasons for this opinion refer to the present political situation of the British Government in India. The missionaries sent to India by nations who have not established any political power in that quarter, have, I conceive, a much better chance of effecting their object than those under other circumstances; but even the Portuguese, the Dutch, the Danes and the French (all of whom endeavoured to establish the Christian religion), were in a situation in India completely different from that in which the British now are. *In the present extended state of our Empire, our security for preserving a power of so extraordinary a nature as that we have established, rests upon the general division of the great communities under the Government, and their subdivision into various castes and tribes; while they continue divided in this manner, no insurrection is likely to shake the stability of our power.* There are but few general motives that could unite communities of men so divided, and many of whom are of a weak and timid character; but it is to be remembered that there is one feeling common almost to them all; that is, an attachment to their religion and prejudices, and this is so strong that I have myself seen it change, in an instant, the lowest, the most timid and most servile Indian into a ferocious barbarian. In a Government so large as that of British India, there must be many who desire its subversion, and who would be ready to employ any means they could to effect that object; such would, I conceive, find those means in any attempt that was made to convert the natives of India, upon a scale that warranted them in a belief it had the encouragement of the British Government. It would not signify to such persons what was the conduct of the missionaries employed, or the tenets of that religion which they taught; their object would be misrepresentation; and they would, I believe, not find it impossible to kindle a flame, which might in its progress not only destroy the British Government, but all who profess the faith it was designed to propagate."

Sir John Malcolm was a past master of diplomacy—both oriental and occidental—a term synonymous with hypocrisy, lying and corruption. He was the biographer of Clive, and knew fully well the principle or principles which guide the British administration of India. From the sentences put in italics in the above, it is clear that he also was of opinion that "*Divide et impera* should be the motto of the Indian Administration." Regarding this point he was more explicit in his evidence before the Select Committee of the House of Commons. He wanted to keep Indians ignorant. He was asked :

"Do not you think that it would be good policy in the British Government to increase the means of information to the natives of India?

In reply he said :

" I consider that in a state of so extraordinary a nature as British India, the first consideration of the Government must always be its own safety; and that the political question of governing that country must be paramount to all other considerations: Under that view of the case, I conceive every subordinate measure (and such I conceive that referred to in the question) must be regulated entirely by the superior consideration of political security.

" Might not an increase in the knowledge of useful arts in the natives, conveyed by British subjects resident in India, tend to strengthen the British Government in India? I conceive that such knowledge might tend in a considerable degree to increase their own comforts and their enjoyment of life; but I cannot see how it would tend in any shape to strengthen the political security of the English Government in India, which appears to me to rest peculiarly upon their present condition."

To explain his meaning more clearly, Sir John Malcolm appeared again of his own accord before the above Committee when he said :

" I wish to add, that I mean by stating that the political security of the British Government in India appears to rest peculiarly upon the present condition of the native subjects, to refer to their actual division into castes, with particular duties and occupations, and to that reverence and respect which they entertain for Europeans, not only on account of their knowledge of the superior branches of science, but also of their better knowledge of many of the mechanical and more useful arts in life; and therefore, though I conceive that the communication of such knowledge to the natives would add to their comforts, and their enjoyments of life, and would increase their strength as a community, I do not think that the communication of any knowledge, which tended gradually to do away the subsisting distinctions among our native subjects or to diminish that respect which they entertain for Europeans, could be said to add to the political strength of the English Government. * * *

"Are not you of opinion, that to increase the comforts and enjoyments of life of the native propulation of India, would tend to strengthen their attachment to the British Government, and consequently to strengthen and insure the stability of that Government in India? From all I have ever been able to observe of nations, I do not think we can calculate upon gratitude for benefits of the nature described as an operating motive that would at all balance against the danger of that strength which such a community as that of our Indian subjects might derive from the general diffusion of knowledge and the eventual abolition of its castes, a consciousness of which would naturally incline them to throw off the yoke of a foreign power; and such they always must consider the British in India; I wish to be understood as alluding in this answer to a danger that is very remote, but yet, in my opinion, worthy of attention.

"Are not the natives of India, in your opinion,

susceptible of gratitude in the highest degree; have you not known instances of generosity and liberality on the part of the natives of India which would have done honor to any man in any age?—I think the natives of India, individually considered, are susceptible of gratitude, and I have known many instances of liberality and generosity among them; but I do not conceive that we can, as I stated before, calculate upon such motives as likely to influence the community, which we shall always find it difficult to rule in proportion as it obtains union and possesses the power of throwing off that subjection in which it is now placed to the British Government."

Mr. Warren Hastings, and especially Sir John Malcolm and others, opposed the introduction of Christian missionaries in India and imparting of knowledge to its inhabitants from considerations of political expediency. But it was on grounds of political expediency, too, that these two measures were advocated.

It was Mr. Charles Grant, described as the Christian Director of the East India Company, who was the first to press upon the British public the expediency of sending Christian missionaries to India for the conversion of its heathen inhabitants, and imparting them education. Charles Grant was in the service of the East India Company in India and was brought up in the school of Clive, Warren Hastings and those Anglo-

Indians of the Eighteenth Century, who according to Burke were "birds of prey and passage in India," and according to Herbert Spencer, "were only a shade less cruel than their prototypes of Peru and Mexico." Like others of his class, he shook the pagoda tree in India, grew rich by amassing a large fortune and then retired on a very handsome pension to England. He took a house at Clapham where he made the acquaintance of Mr. Wilberforce and Mr. Thornton. We read in his biography that Mr. Grant always kept his eye fixed on the chief object of his heart—the evangelisation of India. Having this object in view, he prevailed upon Mr. Wilberforce, when the Company's Charter was about to be renewed in 1793, to introduce two clauses into the Act of Parliament confirming the Charter. These clause ran as follows:

"That it is the peculiar and bounden duty of the Legislature, to promote, by *all just* and *prudent means*, the interests and happiness of the inhabitants of the British dominions in India; and that for these ends, such measures ought to be adopted, as may *gradually* tend to their advancement in *useful knowledge*, and to *their religious and moral improvement*.

"That sufficient means of religious worship and instruction be provided for all persons of the Protestant communion in the service, or under the protection of the East India Company in Asia, proper ministers being from time to time sent out from Great Britain for those purposes;" &c., &c.

Although these two clauses were passed on the first two readings of the Bill, they were rejected on its third reading, because the great body of the East India proprietors, who elected the Directors, were opposed to these clauses for almost the same reasons as those of Mr. Warren Hastings and Sir John Malcolm mentioned above. The following is an abstract of all the arguments, or objections urged against them, as they are reported by Mr. Woodfall.

Objections stated generally :

"That sending missionaries into our Eastern territories, is the most wild, extravagant, expensive, unjustifiable project, that ever was suggested by the most visionary speculator. That the principle is obnoxious, impolitic, unnecessary, full of mischief, dangerous, useless , unlimited."

Specific arguments, *First class :*

"The plan would be dangerous and impolitic; it would affect the peace and ultimate security of our possessions. It tends to endanger and injure our affairs there most fatally, it would either produce disturbances, or bring the Christian religion into contempt. Holding one faith or religion, is the most strong common cause with mankind, and the moment that took place in India there would be an end of British supremacy.

"That the principle of proselyting was *impolitic*, and was, or ought to be exploded, in so enlightened a period as the eighteenth century.

"That it would be a most serious and fatal disaster, if natives of character, even a hundred thousand of them, were converted to Christianity.

"That the establishment of seminaries and colleges in America, was one of the most efficient causes of the loss of that country.

"That suffering young clergymen, (who are usually of pleasureable habits), to overrun the interior of India, would be dangerous, and prove ultimately destructive to the Company's interest."

Second class :

"The scheme would be unsuccessful. It is extravagant to hope for the conversion of the natives. They are invincibly attached to their own castes; their prejudices, manners, and habits, are all against a change.

"It is vain to attempt to overcome prejudices fixed by the practice of ages, far exceeding the time in which Britons had any idea of religion at all. The attempt is, in these views, idle, absurd, and impracticable.

"Only the dregs of the people can be converted; they will pretend conversion, and disgrace Christianity.

"The higher and more respectable natives, are people of the purest morality, and strictest virtue.

"The services of religion are devoutly performed in the Company's settlements and ships, either by clergymen or laymen, and their ecclesiastical establishments are sufficient."

Third class :

"*The scheme would be expensive.* The expense would be enormous, intolerable; one, two, or three hundred thousand pounds."

Fourth class :

"The scheme would be unlimited, in respect of the numbers and qualifications of the missionaries."

European Christians in general and natives of England more especially are not remarkable for being strict in the observance and practice of the tenets of their religion or for their spread. They were not like the Muhammadans or even the Roman Catholics of the fifteenth and sixteenth centuries—the authors of the Holy Inquisition—desirous of making converts. The natives of England understand the pleasures, comforts and conveniences of this world. They as a nation do not seem to care much for the Other World and, therefore, do not trouble themselves for saving the souls of other peoples. It was on these grounds then that the clauses in the Charter Bill of 1793, respecting sending missionaries to India and educating its inhabitants, were not passed.

Mr. Grant was not greatly disappointed. He tried to become a director of the East India

Company and was elected on May 30, 1794. He also entered Parliament in 1802. Whether in the India House or in Parliament he exerted the influence which he wielded in inducing his countrymen to allow missionaries and school-masters to proceed to India in order to convert and enlighten its heathen population. He wrote a pamphlet entitled,

"Observations on the state of Society among the *Asiatic* subjects of *Great Britain*, particularly with respect to Morals; and on the means of improving it."

This was meant to refute the arguments of those who were opposed to sending Christian missionaries to India. In order to succeed in his endeavour, he had to appeal to the two classes of his countrymen, *viz.*, those who professed or pretended to be philanthropists, and secondly, the men of the world, which constituted by far the larger class of his countrymen, with whom "£. *s. d.* is their Trinity." To appeal to the philanthropic instinct of his countrymen, he did what the Christian missionaries are in the habit of doing to this day, that is, vilifying, and painting the natives of India in the blackest colour possible. No unprejudiced man knowing anything of the character of the Hindoos would or could say that the chapters in the pamphlet regarding "view of the Morals of the Hindoos" and "causes of the situation and character of the Hindoos" are a fair, just or correct estimate of the character of the Hindoos. He very wantonly attacked them and painted them in the blackest colour possible, which was not fair. He had to serve his purpose and it seems to us that he did so on the principle of the end justifying the means.

However, in appealing to the philanthropic instinct of his countrymen, he was obliged to refer to the dark side of the British administration of India. He wrote :

"All the offices of trust, civil and military, and the first lines of commerce, are in the hands of foreigners, who after a temporary residence remove with their acquisitions in constant succession. The government is foreign. Of *native* rulers, even the *rapacious* exactions went again into circulation, and the tribute formerly paid to Delhi, passing chiefly by the medium of private commerce, when a general communication throughout the Empire gave Bengal great advantages, was little felt. But the tribute paid to us extracts every year a large portion of the produce of that country without the least return. * *

"These observations, and the review which precedes them, are intended forcibly to impress upon the mind the sense of those peculiar obligations under which we lie to the people of our Asiatic territories, on account of benefits we draw from them, the disadvantages they have suffered, and must still in certain ways suffer from their connection with us, and the relation in which they stand to us as our subjects. * * * * In decreeing that our subjects shall be delivered from oppression and injustice, in setting an equitable limit to our own demands, and in establishing rights of property * *, have we done all that the circumstances of the Hindoos require, all that is incumbent upon us as rulers? * * * * We ought also to remember how much the authority of a handful of strangers depends on *opinion.* To reduce the sources of prejudice against us, and to multiply impressions favourable to us, by assimilating our subjects to our modes of thinking, and by making them happy, and teaching them to understand and value the principles of the people who confer happiness upon them, may be some of the surest means of preserving the footing we have acquired."

Even from the above extract it will be noticed that it was not purely philanthropic or altruistic considerations which prompted Mr. Charles Grant to advocate the sending of Christian missionaries to India and the imparting of instruction to its inhabitants. His philanthropy or altruism was largely tempered or rather alloyed with selfish motives. This will be evident from the extracts from his pamphlet which we give below.

The mask of philanthropy which Mr. Charles Grant put on, when he advocated the evangelisation and education of the heathens of India was not the one calculated to inspire confidence in his co-religionists and compatriots. Therefore, in order to convince his countrymen that it would pay them if natives of India were educated and also converted to Christianity, he was obliged to remove the mask and appear in his real character. Towards the end of the pamphlet referred to above, he wrote, "Wherever, we may venture to say, our principles and language are introduced, our commerce will follow."

Here, at last, the cat is out of the bag. This convinced the Christian natives of England more forcibly than all the arguments which had been advanced from philanthropic considerations for the education and conversion of heathens. Again he wrote :

> "By planting our language, our knowledge, our opinions, and our religion, in our Asiatic territories, we shall put a great work beyond the reach of contingencies; we shall probably have wedded the inhabitants of those territories to this country."

That is quite true. The Christian nations and countries of the West send missionaries of their faith to non-Christian nations, not so much for the spiritual welfare of the latter, as for the worldly good which these missionaries bring to the Christian nations.

That Indian patriot, Lala Lajpat Rai, who was deported out of India without any trial and without knowing the nature of the charges preferred against him, and over whose deportation almost the whole of the Christian Anglo-Indians —whether clergymen or lay men—greatly rejoiced, wrote in one of his letters from America, which he visited in 1905 :

"The other day there was held a conference of missionaries in which President Copen is said to have advocated the extension of the mission work for the benefit of the American trade. I cull the following report from the *Boston Advertiser*:—'Save the world to save America' was the theme of the annual address of President Copen. He said, in part, we need to develop foreign missions to save our nation commercially. * * * * It is only as we develop missions that we shall have a market in the Orient which will demand our manufactured articles in sufficient quantities to match our increased facilities. The Christian man is our customer. The heathen has, as a rule, few wants. It is only when man is changed that there comes this desire for the manifold articles that belonged to the Christian man and the Christian home. *The missionary is everywhere and always the pioneer of trade*'."

Commenting on the above extract, Lala Lajpat Rai very rightly observed :

"The Indian admirers and friends of Christian missions ought to note this commercial ideal of the American missionary. The missionary is not 'the pioneer of trade' only but also the pioneer of the political supremacy of the Boston people in the East.

I think that the frank statement of leading Christians ought to open the eyes of all who see no danger in the work of the Christian Missions in the East.

If truth be told, it must be admitted that Christian nations are not anxious to save the souls of the heathens but wish to enrich themselves, and, therefore, send missionaries to non-Christian lands.

Mr. Charles Grant, although he called himself a Christian, did not perhaps believe in the brotherhood of man. He was in favour of converting and educating the heathens of India, but certainly he was not in favour of giving them any political rights and privileges. The chief argument against the diffusion of useful knowledge amongst, and conversion to Christianity of, the natives of India, was that they would demand independence and throw off the yoke of England. Mr. Charles Grant thought otherwise, for he wrote :

"The great danger with which the objector alarms us is, that the communication of the Gospel and of European light, may probably be introductive of a popular form of Government and the assertion of independence. Upon what grounds is it inferred, that these effects must follow in any case, especially in the most unlikely case of the Hindoos? The establishment of Christianity in a country does not necessarily bring after it a free political constitution. The early

Christians made no attempts to change forms of Government; the spirit of the Gospel does not encourage even any disposition which might lead to such attempts. Christianity has been long the religion of many parts of Europe and of various protestant states, where the form of Government is not popular. It is its peculiar excellence, and an argument of its intended universality, that it may subsist under different forms of Government, and in all render men happy, and even societies flourishing; * * It does not, in the pursuit of these objects, erect a peculiar political system; it views politics through the safe medium of morals." * *

We do not wish to enter into the discussion whether Christianity can or has the power of uplifting any people. But this much is evident that Mr. Charles Grant did not believe in the Rights of Man which Thomas Paine, a pronounced non-Christian, did. How can a religion make a man happy and prosperous, if he is not allowed to have some share in the good things of this world? Our Christian friends are very anxious to save our souls, but at the same time wish to keep us slaves. The words of the Italian patriot, Joseph Mazzini, should be poured into the ears of these good Christians. Mazzini wrote :

"Is it then by leaving man in the hands of his oppressors that you would elevate and emancipate his soul? Is it by leaving erect the Idol of blind Force, in the service of Imposture, that you think to raise in the human soul an altar to the God of a free conscience?"

Yes, Mr. Charles Grant wanted to keep the natives of India perpetually under the leading strings of his own countrymen. He wrote that,

"We can foresee no period in which we may not govern our Asiatic subjects, more happily for them than they can be governed by themselves or any other power; and doing this *we should not expose them to needless danger from without and from within, by giving the military power into their hands.*"

Mr. Charles Grant was a Christian and believed in the "Brotherhood of Man!"

According to him, neither conversion to Christianity nor imparting of instruction to the natives was calculated to inspire them with any desire for liberty. He wrote :

"Where then is the rational ground for apprehending that such a race will ever become turbulent for English liberty? A spirit of English liberty is not to be caught from a written description of it, by distant and feeble Asiatics especially. It was not originally conceived nor conveyed by a theoretical scheme. It has grown in the succession of ages from the active exertions of the human powers; and perhaps can be relished only by a people thus prepared. Example is more likely to inspire a taste for it than report; but the nations of Europe have seen that liberty and its great effects, without being led to imitation of it; for the

French Revolution proceeds not upon its principles; it is an eruption of atheism and anarchy.

"The English inhabiting our settlements in India, have no share in the British Government. Some are employed as servants of the public, but no one possesses any legislative right. Why then should we give to the natives, even if they aspired to it, as it is unlikely that they will thus aspire, what we properly refuse to our own people? The British inhabitants would be extremely averse to such a participation."

Such were the views of this model Christian according to whom Indians should be looked upon as foes and aliens in the land of their birth, and as helots who ought not to possess any rights and privileges.

We need not quote any further from the writings of this man. It was he by whose endeavour were introducted in the Charter Act of 1813 those clauses permitting missionaries to proceed to India, establishing the Ecclesiastical Department at the expense of the natives of India, although it did not benefit them in the least, and also made the authorities of the East India Company set apart one lakh of rupees for the instruction of the natives of India. Neither Charles Grant nor the natives of England were prompted by any motive of philanthropy or altruism to grant these measures to India. It was sordid considerations of worldly gain which led the people of England to adopt the above measures under the cloak of philanthropy.

It was political expediency which was at the bottom of the desire of the natives of England for the conversion of the heathens of India. This is quite clear from what Mr. Charles Grant wrote, extracts from whose writings have already been given above. We are borne out in our view of the case by the writings of another Englishman who possessed the reputation of being a very zealous Christian. The name of this Englishman is Mr. William Edwards. He served in India during the Indian Mutiny, after which event, he rose to be a Judge of Her Majesty's High Court of Agra. In 1866, he published his "Reminiscences of a Bengal Civilian." In the last chapter of his work, he says :

"We *are*, and ever must be, regarded as foreign invaders and conquerors, and the more the people become enlightened and civilised the more earnest will, in all probability, be their efforts to get rid of us. Our best safeguard is in the evangelization of the country; for although Christianity does not denationalize, its spread would be gradual, and Christian settlements scattered about the country would be as towers of strength for many years to come, for *they* must be loyal so long as the mass of the people remain either idolators or Mahomedans."*

* P. 336.

Considerations like the above must have influenced the English—a nation of shopkeepers —in favour of the conversion of the natives of India. They were told that the presence of the Christian missionaries in India would not contribute to the happiness of its inhabitants. The missionaries are as a class very aggressive, and wantonly outrage the religious susceptibilities of others who do not subscribe to their dogmas and tenets. This leads not very rarely to bloodshed even. This is exactly what was anticipated in India by those who were opposed to the Christian Missions. But perhaps the scheming and designing politicians of England thought that such a state of affairs would keep India under the control of England. The missionaries by exasperating the heathens provoke breaches of the peace, but they are not punished but the heathens. We see this tragedy or comedy being enacted every day in non-Christian countries. Lufcadio Hearn, Lecturer on English Literature in the University of Tokyo, says :

"Force, the principal instrument of Christian propagandism in the past, is still the force behind our mission. Only we have, or affect to have, substituted money-power or menace for the franker edge of the sword; occasionally fulfilling the menace for commercial reasons in proof of our Christian professions. We force missionaries upon China, for example, under treaty-clauses extorted by war, and pledge ourselves to support them with gun-boats and to exact enormous indemnities for the lives of such as get themselves killed. So China pays blood-money at regular intervals, and is learning more and more each year the value of what we call Christianity."

In his despatch presented to Parliament in March 1895, Sir Gerald Portal said :

"The race for converts, now being carried on by the Romish and Protestant missionaries in Uganda, is synonymous with the race for political power. That the missionaries on both sides are the veritable political leaders of their respective factions, there can be no doubt whatever. The Romish Fathers would admit this to be the case; on the Protestant side, it would not be admitted, but the fact unfortunately remains. The three great parties of Islam, Rome and Protestantism, though nominally only divided by religious tenets, are in reality adverse and jealous political camps, and the leadership of two of these camps is practically in the hands of European missionaries."

Mr. George Nathaniel (afterwards Lord) Curzon wrote in the *National Review* for 1893 :

"Without hostility to the missionaries, it is impossible to ignore the fact that English missionaries are a source of political unrest and frequently of international trouble, subversive of the national institutions of a country in which they reside."

But India is a land of toleration. Here the

Christian missionaries have not been so roughly handled as they seem to have been in some other non-Christian countries. So the schemes of the designing politicans of England have been to some extent frustrated in India at least.

The people of India, although they do not owe allegiance to Christ, are saturated through and through, with those principles which Christ preached. They do not and never did stand in need of Christian missionaries. On the contrary, it is the Christian islanders, whether natives of England or Scotland, who very sadly required the ministrations of their clergymen. The amount of immorality which prevails in those Christian countries is simply appalling. Debauchery, drunkenness, in short every sort of crime and vice, grows and thrives luxuriantly in the soil of Christian England and Scotland. General Booth was not wrong in branding large portions of the land of his birth and living as "Darkest England." So when we find the natives of that country, instead of trying to remove the darkness that overspreads their own homes, sending missions to other lands, we must naturally conclude that they must have some other ulterior motives in view, and not merely the salvation of the souls of the dark heathens.

Thus it was selfish and certainly not philanthropic considerations which prompted the people of England to send Christian missions to India and impart instruction to the natives.

Christian missionaries who are sent out to heathen lands do not seem to care so much for the welfare of the souls of the dark-skinned races as to bring those lands under the subjugation of Christian powers by stirring up troubles in those lands. Thus in the *Saturday Review* of July 10, 1880, in an article under the title of "flogging missionaries," it is said :

"The sovereign authority which missionaries are said to claim over uncivilised tribes, the missionary right to try, condemn, torture, flog, imprison, and starve, are very serious matters. Almost all our recent 'little wars' have sprung, more or less directly, from the enterprise of missionaries. The Abyssinian affair was caused by missionaries. Missionaries spread the reports about Cetewayo's cruelty and contempt of the Sabbath day, which at least hastened the perhaps inevitable encounter with the Zulus. A missionary complicated the relations of the late Government with the Porte, and missionaries have interfered pretty freely with the domestic Royal quarrels which keep Burmah in hot water. Mr. Stanley's expedition, no doubt, was a journalistic, not a religious one. He converted a casual King or two by the way, but his real end was to increase the circulation of the *Daily Telegraph* and the *New York Herald*. If he shot negroes in so noble a cause it would scarcely be fair to credit missionaries with his victories over naked enemies."

It is not necessary to quote more from the above article to show the doings of Christian Missionaries in heathen lands. But the state of affairs revealed in the above extract is not calculated to credit Christian Missions with the desire to advance the cause of the uplift of humanity.

BIBLIOGRAPHY.

I. Parliamentary Papers.

(*a*) Minutes of evidence taken before the Select Committee on the affairs of the East India Company, Vol. I, Public. Ordered, by the House of Commons, to be printed, 16th Aug., 1832.

(*b*) Ditto, Ditto, Vol. VI, Political. Ditto.

(*c*) Sixth Report from the Select Committee on Indian territories, 1853.

(*d*) East India (Education) ordered by the House of Commons to be printed, 11th August, 1859.

(1) Bengal & N.-W. P.

(2) Madras.

(3) Bombay.

II. Macaulay's Minute published in Macmillan's Magazine for 1864.

III. Raja Ram Mohun Roy's letter to Lord Amherst in the English works of Raja Ram Mohun Roy, published by the Panini Office, Allahabad.

IV. Hunter's Education Commission of 1882. Report and Minutes of Evidence.

V. Sadler's Calcutta University Commission of 1920. Report and Minutes of Evidence in 13 Vols.

VI. Syed Mahmud's History of English Education in India, 1781-1893.

VII. Prof. Holman's English National Education.

VIII. The Calcutta Review (Old Series), The Modern Review, &c., &c.